YOUR NEXT CHAPTER

YOUR
NEXT
CHAPTER

A Woman's Guide To A Successful Retirement

Alexandra Armstrong CFP®
Mary R. Donahue Ph.D.

For information about this title, electronic media or to
order other books, contact the publisher:

"On Your Own Publishing Company LLC"
1800 M Street NW, Suite 1010-S,
Washington DC 20036
Website: https://your-nextchapter.com
yournextchapterauthors@gmail.com

ISBN: 978-1-7341575-0-5 (print)
978-1-7341575-1-2 (eBook)

Library of Congress Control Number: 2019920493

Printed in the United States of America

Cover design: Longview Strategies
Interior design: 1106 Design

Publisher's Cataloging-In-Publication Data
(Prepared by The Donohue Group, Inc.)
Names: Armstrong, Alexandra, author. | Donahue, Mary R., author.
Title: Your next chapter : a woman's guide to a successful retirement / Alexandra
Armstrong, CFP, [and] Mary R. Donahue, Ph.D.
Description: Washington DC : On Your Own Publishing Company LLC, [2020] |
Includes index.
Identifiers: ISBN 9781734157505 (print) | ISBN 9781734157512 (ebook)
Subjects: LCSH: Women--Retirement--Psychological aspects. | Women--Retirement--
Economic aspects. | Older women--Finance, Personal.
Classification: LCC HQ1062 .A76 2020 (print) | LCC
HQ1062 (ebook) | DDC 306.38082--dc23

This publication is designed to provide accurate and authoritative information in regard
to the subject matter covered. It is sold with the understanding that the authors are not
engaged in rendering legal, accounting, or other professional services by publishing this
book. As each individual situation is unique, questions relevant to personal finances and
specific to the individual should be addressed to an appropriate professional to ensure
that the situation has been evaluated carefully and appropriately. The authors specifically
disclaim any liability, loss or risk which is incurred as a consequence, directly or indirectly,
of the use and application of any of the contents of this book.

This book is dedicated to all the women who are on the
brink of retirement and are wrestling with
all the decisions they need to make.

Table Of Contents

Preface

Retirement is a major life event. As with any major life transition, you're likely to be anxious or perhaps even uneasy, especially if there are no established rules or guidelines. These days, retirement can be particularly unsettling, given the emotional and financial changes it brings. We believe that many people, particularly women, haven't adequately planned emotionally for this new chapter in their lives. This makes the retirement planning process even more complex.

We think the term "RETIREMENT" is a misnomer. According to Webster's Dictionary: "to retire is to remove oneself from the scene" and by implication disappear. Indeed, you may be leaving whatever it was you were doing throughout the majority of your adult life (paid or unpaid), but you're not moving into a state of oblivion. Rather you're about to begin a new chapter in the ongoing story of your life. In this newest phase of your life you have choices to make and forward motion to embrace. It's a stage of life like any other stage you experience. Some of you will be able to move ahead with enthusiasm. Others will view it tentatively. Unfortunately, others may consider it the end of life and experience feelings of uselessness and depression and anxiety, sometimes leading to a sense of paralysis in a world of unknowns.

In this book we explore retirement as women writing for women, cognizant of all that is before you. Both of us have struggled with the concept of retirement. Although we have written a book about retirement for women based on our experiences, we have chosen to delay full retirement past the traditional retirement age. We both are fortunate enough to be in professions which allow us to do this since we run our own practices. While we no longer are working full-time, we gradually have reduced our workloads, thus gliding slowly into what is considered retirement.

Why did we make this personal choice? Our primary motivator was that we like what we do. We find our professional lives stimulating and rewarding. We enjoy the socialization as well as the challenges our work provides and are able to control our own schedules. So as long as our minds and our bodies are functioning well, we intend to stay involved to some extent. Based on our interactions with our clients and friends we realize that we aren't typical. However, at the same time, we're very aware of the complexities of retirement. The emotional and physical components are intertwined with the financial aspects and the experience is different for women than for men.

Our own life experiences and struggles with the meaning of retirement have motivated us to write this book for all women, hoping they will benefit from our personal journey and those of our clients and friends. All of our data reinforces the fact that the need to continue to feel useful is universal, as is the need to enrich our lives and minds.

We acknowledge the potential emotional peaks and valleys you will face when you retire, but it's our belief that retirement is an evolving process. It's our goal that this book will help you create a personal and rewarding one.

Over the past 75 years, women's roles in society have dramatically changed in ways that hadn't been imagined. Women started working outside of the home in World War II, when it was necessary for them to join the workforce and take on jobs traditionally undertaken by men while the men served in the military. This was the start of the female revolution in the job market. Prior to this time, most employed women worked out of necessity in jobs usually assumed by women, such as teaching or nursing. After the war, many women found they liked working, for several reasons. They enjoyed the work, they contributed to the family income and their salary also provided them with some financial independence.

In the 1950s, although more women graduated from college than ever before, their employment options were limited. The primary available choices continued to be as teachers, nurses and secretaries. In the 1960s, the first oral birth control pill was approved for distribution, which increased women's life choices. Over time, the number of women attending and graduating from college has steadily progressed, to the point that today women outnumber men in college. By 2016, more women were graduating from law school than men and were close to outnumbering men in medical school. Today, women are in leadership positions as CEOs of major corporations, managing partners in law firms, senators, governors, respected physicians and high-ranking officers in the military to name but a few.

These societal factors have led to a change in the way women look at their lives. Studies consistently show that despite a woman's role in the work environment she still is likely to assume the primary responsibility for the children—if she has children—and family life in general.

After years of juggling work and family obligations successfully many women find it difficult to envision a life where their role is not defined by some outside demand or expected role. This may lead to many conflicted emotions.

For the first time in history professional women are facing some of the same issues men have primarily addressed with regard to leaving the workforce but with more complicated components. Most men enter the workforce anticipating that they will work for a certain number of years and then retire. Such is not the case with women. When their careers in the workplace and their familiar roles within the family are terminating at around the same time many women are left feeling adrift. Compounding these feelings is the recognition that the demands of daily life had not left much time or energy for embracing this new stage of life. This is equally true for the non-working woman whose life is dramatically changed by the planned (or unplanned) retirement of her partner.

Many of these women are healthy, have enjoyed what they have done for a living and derived satisfaction from their careers and family involvement. This new chapter may not provide these women with the same type of satisfaction and recognition they experienced when working outside the home and assuming ongoing family roles, but it should provide a new freedom of choice not available in the past. In addition to all of these emotional factors, there is the financial component—women live longer than men and therefore their money has to last longer.

Women come to this new chapter in their lives from different places. Some have been working throughout their adult lives, enjoyed what they did but are ready to leave the job market. Others tolerated work and are anxious to be done with the life of the working woman whatever that brings. Still others obtained considerable satisfaction from their careers and are having a difficult time letting go of the rewards in terms of how they have defined themselves. Lastly, there are the women whose lives are about to be altered by changes in their partners' lives as they retire.

In the first part of this book we help you as a woman assess your own financial, emotional and physical situation as you plan for your imminent retirement and the choices that you need to make. In the second part, we evaluate how you may adjust to your first year of retirement. The initial financial decisions you make in some cases are irrevocable and will impact the rest of your lives. Others are not. It's most important to understand which decisions fall into which category. However, this is not a simple task as one's emotional state and physical health play a major role in one's decision making. These three aspects form the whole and influence all of one's ultimate choices. It would be nice if we could put these factors into compartments, but unfortunately such is not the reality.

To illustrate the choices women about to retire have to make, we've created fictional (yet we believe realistic) stories of four women facing different aspects of retirement in various regions of the country. We follow these women in each chapter of our book as they first assess their situation and then adjust to this new chapter in their lives.

These women are:

*C*atherine: a partner in a law firm in Washington, DC, whose husband has just been told that his company has been sold and his position has been eliminated.

*E*mily: a divorcee in Atlanta, Georgia, working for a nonprofit organization and struggling with personal money issues.

She is concerned about her adult son and her new personal relationship.

Melissa: a homemaker in a Detroit suburb who has assumed considerable family responsibilities while at the same time dealing with a husband who wants them to move to a warmer climate when he retires.

Victoria: a single, tenured professor in Berkeley, California, trying to envision how she'll fill her time when she retires.

One final note: Since this book is written by women for women we have used "she" when referring to the various advisors, although we realize some of your advisors may be male.

Part One

Assessing Your Current Situation
Before You Retire

CHAPTER ONE

Women's Profiles

CATHERINE: FACTUAL PROFILE

Age:	59
Occupation:	Estate Planning Lawyer
Marital Status:	Married to Jordan, age 63
Husband's occupation:	Corporate attorney for small private company
Years married:	35 years
Children:	James, age 30, architect
	Amanda, age 28, applying to law school
Parents:	Mary and Fred, early 80s, living in nearby apartment, in good health
	His father, Ben, age 92, widower, lives in New Jersey.
Her Siblings:	Judy, age 54

His Siblings:	None
Financial Planner:	Joe Schwartz
Employment Counselor:	Judy Byrne
Realtor Friend:	Jessica Johnson
Health:	Both good
Residence:	Chevy Chase, Maryland, 10 years left on mortgage
	2nd home in Bethany Beach, Delaware, no mortgage
Investments:	Jordan and Catherine have 401(k) accounts as well as a joint portfolio.
Financial Lifestyle:	Casual about finances but not big spenders

CATHERINE: DESCRIPTIVE CHARACTER PROFILE

Monday morning. Catherine was back at the office early as usual. She poured herself a cup of coffee and sat down at her desk. She glanced at the cherry wood bookcases that held her many law books and references. It was so comfortable and familiar. She felt more at home at the office these days than at home. Ever since Jordan had been told that his company had been sold and he was facing early retirement everything seemed to have changed. She wondered why she and Jordan had never spent any time thinking and talking about what they would do when they were no longer working. With no warning, they now had to face the fact that Jordan was about to be forced into retirement as a result of his company being sold where he had worked for over 25 years.

She shook her short blond hair, took off her conservative black pinstripe jacket and turned her dark brown eyes to the Turner file that was in front of her on her desk. She was supposed to meet with the Turners later today. She found herself saying to herself, "Come on, Catherine, you don't have to resolve all your family issues in a day or a weekend!" but somehow, she couldn't shake off the nagging thoughts of where the time had gone. Were they really at an age where they needed to be thinking about retirement? What did that word "retirement" mean anyway? She had only made partner five years ago. She loved what she did, but what if she was working and Jordan was at home not working. How would that impact their relationship?

Catherine and Jordan had met at Georgetown Law School in Washington, DC, which was a far cry from her undergraduate life at Bowdoin College in Maine. Back then everything about Washington, DC, excited her. It was the same for Jordan, a tall lanky guy with sandy blonde hair and gray eyes from Cherry Hill, New Jersey. His clothes never seemed to fit just right. His sleeves were too short and his jackets rumpled.

They had met one evening at the law library during her first year in law school. She remembered being frustrated by a case she was having trouble understanding. He had seen her frowning at the page in front of her. From across the table he awkwardly cleared his throat and said, "Maybe I can help you." He was a second-year law student and she had just started law school. Sometimes she still felt like that same shy girl, but mostly not.

Catherine and Jordan began to spend time together doing casual things and studying. Neither one of them wanted to rush into anything serious. She had a number of girlfriends that she enjoyed spending time with, and he was busy with school and work.

After graduating from Rutgers University in New Jersey, he went to work for the New Jersey Transportation Department. He worked there for two years and saved his money so he could afford to go to law school. He was very financially responsible and needed to feel that he could pay his own way. She liked that about him.

She realized that he had always made her feel secure and protected. Just being with Jordan calmed her down. She'd been content to let him take care of their finances. After so many years at one company, now that he was about to be out of work, what did their future look like? There were so many unanswered questions.

They had married at the Georgetown University Chapel after she graduated from law school and he was working for a law firm dealing with government contracts. How excited she'd been with her newly married life. They had a small group of friends with whom they shared picnics, barbecues, walks in Georgetown along the canal, Redskin games, and everything else their city had to offer.

For the first five years of their marriage they worked for different law firms and on different aspects of the law. They shared their individual successes and frustrations experienced in the work environment. They'd agreed they wanted to have two children and were ecstatic when they found out she was pregnant. When James was born he was greeted enthusiastically. Jordan and she agreed she would return to work after a three-month maternity leave. Between their two salaries, they could afford to have a nanny. Catherine loved being a mother but also enjoyed the intellectual challenge of work.

Two years later, she gave birth to Amanda. At that point Jordan was doing very well financially. Catherine was torn between being an at-home mother and continuing on her path to partnership at the law firm. Jordan left the final decision to her. Ultimately they agreed on her resigning from the firm to stay home with the children during their formative years. Life just seemed to bump along. Twenty years ago, they moved to a bigger house. She did her share of volunteer work related to the children's lives and activities. She was always a classroom mother, and she had been a PTA president as well as a Brownie leader. The time had flown by!

Catherine had valued the opportunity to socialize with the parents of the children's friends. In fact, they'd remained friends with two of the couples they'd met through the children's activities. However, she had to admit she never did get into cooking the way many of her friends did.

When she turned 47 and felt the children were well able to manage their school work and extracurricular activities with minimal assistance from her, with some trepidation she and Jordan had agreed that she could return to work. It had been 13 years since she had worked outside the home. She truly loved the law and particularly her field of estate planning. Although she had been at home all that time, she'd kept up with developments in her field and thus was able to reinstate herself at her former firm.

She smiled to herself. Here she was helping others with their estate plans, but she never gave much thought to the fact that she and Jordan were getting older and needed to plan for their own retirement and create an estate plan. She thought that old expression about the shoemaker's children applied to them.

After five years back at the law firm she made partner. She felt good about it. It seemed to her she was in the prime of her life. Now, at age 60, her work life was going well. Their children had graduated from college and were doing well on their own. James was working with an architectural firm in the area and recently had been given a plum assignment as the lead architect developing a large multi-use project that would include offices, varied housing options as well as stores and restaurants in Washington, DC. In addition, for the past two years he'd been dating a lovely young woman working in the real estate field. It did look as though they were moving in the direction of marriage, which pleased both Catherine and Jordan.

Amanda had worked in retail for the first few years after she had graduated from college but had decided the field wasn't right for her long-term. For the past two years she'd been working for a DC law firm, which had sparked her interest in the law and motivated her to apply to law school.

Catherine served on two nonprofit boards. One was the Girl Scouts, which she'd initially been involved with when Amanda was a Brownie. The other was Reading is Fundamental, which focused on motivating young children to read. She enjoyed this volunteer work as well as her work-related activities. She realized she wasn't ready to retire. How was all this going to work out?

What about Jordan? In the past, they'd had no trouble discussing all sorts of things as well as their feelings and reaching mutual decisions. It was something she'd always valued, but when Jordan was told by the owner of his company that he was selling and the new owners would be making sweeping changes, he seemed to have shut down. These changes included the elimination of his job. After all those years working for the same company did he feel that his life was over? Did he feel like less of a man? She couldn't imagine that. Occasionally they had talked about what life might be like when they were retired, but those conversations were very superficial and retirement always seemed so far off that it didn't really require their attention.

They had fantasized about what they might like to do when they were no longer working and had more free time. However, they never talked about how much this would cost and had no concept of how their financial situation might look like when they retired. It was fun to imagine a time in their lives when they were not working, but right now they both enjoyed what they were doing so much that they had been in no rush to retire.

EMILY: FACTUAL PROFILE

Age:	64
Occupation:	Executive director of a small nonprofit
Marital status:	Divorced from Doug, age 75
His occupation:	Ad agency executive
Years married:	26
Children:	Jill, age 38, married to Garrett, Lives in Durham, North Carolina
	2 children: Angela (12) and Troy (10)
	Carter age 35, has ADHD and currently lives with Emily
Boyfriend:	Hank, age 66, divorced for 3 years
	Son Harvey (40) and 2 grandchildren: Tracey (16) and Olivia (14)
	Lives in an apartment.
	He is a partner in a mid-size local accounting firm
Parents:	Her father deceased, mother Serah, a widow, age 85
Siblings:	None
Financial Planner:	Shelley Stone
Realtor:	Amy Johnson
Yoga Friend:	Carla
Health:	Chronic back problem but otherwise healthy
Residence:	Marital home in Atlanta, Georgia, no mortgage
Investments:	Pension plan from Doug and her own retirement account
Financial Lifestyle:	Lives within her current income with occasional splurges

EMILY: DESCRIPTIVE CHARACTER PROFILE

The whir of the lawn care company's large lawn mowers awakened her. It was Saturday morning. Why did they always seem to need to mow the grass on a Saturday morning? She'd asked them to schedule the lawn work during the week, but it didn't seem to matter. They did what was convenient for them. Oh well. She would rather stay in bed for a while longer, but she knew she had a great deal to do today, so it would probably be wise to get up and get going on her "to do" list.

When she and Doug divorced 10 years ago after three years of separation, she had been very pleased that he hadn't given her a hard time about her wanting to keep the marital home. She wanted the children to have the security of knowing that they could always return to the home where they had grown up. Sometimes, like now, she questioned the wisdom of that decision. Back then, she had her hands full processing what had happened to her marriage.

Emily and Doug had met when she was a hotel management major in graduate school. She obtained an internship in the administrative offices of a major hotel chain where he was the senior person in the office. She was honored that he wanted to be so helpful to her in understanding the many aspects of the hotel business. She remembered always being very prompt when arriving at work with her jet black, long hair tied neatly in a ponytail and her very dark eyes lightly made up.

One day Doug asked her to stay late and complete a project that had been assigned to her. When she was finished and the others had all left, he'd asked if she would like to have a drink with him. Feeling flattered, she had said yes. One thing had led to another and he ended up taking her home after an extended dinner. He told her how much he'd enjoyed her company. He didn't think it appropriate for them to date while she was working as an intern at the hotel, but if it was okay with her, he would like to take her out again at the end of her internship. She was beyond pleased.

She wasn't sure what he saw in her, since he was ten years older than she was, but he always made her feel special and they had many interests in common. They were both avid tennis players and loved to be out on the water when they could manage it. He belonged to a country club, and soon they were playing doubles on a regular basis. According to him, he'd been engaged before he met her, but after a long engagement his fiancée had broken it off.

It would be fair to say that he swept her off her feet. When he proposed to her over a champagne dinner at the club, she was ecstatic. Their parents liked each other enormously. She had the perfect wedding with all the trimmings and excitedly embraced married life. He told her that he didn't care if she worked or not. He made enough money to support his wife and the children he wanted to have. Given his age, he was actually anxious to be a father.

It wasn't long before she became pregnant and had Jill. She was an easy baby and her friends were all jealous of the attention Doug lavished on her and the baby. She dressed Jill up like a doll. Three years later along came Carter. That was a rude awakening. He was fussy from day one—often crying when it wasn't clear what would soothe him. In all honesty he'd always been a problem and still was one in some ways. She often felt that after they had had Carter, life changed. Doug wanted to live an ideal life. He had an image of what life should be like whether or not that was the case. They had always enjoyed an active sex life, but after Carter was born sometimes she was just too tired to be sexually available to Doug in bed. Now she believed he had felt rejected and was unable to accept that she had to meet the children's needs and wasn't always available for him as she had been in the past. She hadn't understood any of that at the time.

Carter had many learning issues. He was diagnosed with ADHD at an early age. He always needed to have special accommodations at school and extra tutoring. Doug didn't know how to react to Carter and their relationship had always been strained. Carter wasn't well coordinated and as a result couldn't share Doug's interests in tennis or any other sport for that matter.

When both children were in school, Emily decided to go back to work. She wanted to have a meaningful job, not just collect a paycheck. Therefore she went to work for a non-profit which provided educational services to disadvantaged children. Since it was a nonprofit she didn't make as much money as she might have made in the corporate world, but she always felt useful and that she was making a difference in these children's lives.

When spring was in the air, she often found herself thinking about her earlier life with Doug. He had divorced her ten year earlier for a much younger woman who worked for him as an event planner. Emily wondered if he had given her the same line that he'd given her that allowed her to fall for him so many years ago. She didn't hate Doug. Mainly she was disappointed. In her opinion they could have gone to a marriage counselor and worked things out but he would have none of it.

Her daughter, Jill, was really doing well. She and Garrett seemed to have a solid marriage. Their two children seemed to be thriving both in school and in their extracurricular activities. Carter, on the other hand, continued to struggle, and her heart broke for him. He'd had years and years of therapy but still had major self-esteem issues. He knew he was a disappointment to his father, but he continued to work to get his attention and make him proud. He'd like to be married. He'd had several girlfriends but none of these relationships had worked out.

Emily turned her thoughts to Hank. Two years ago, they had been introduced to each other by a mutual friend. When they met, Hank had been divorced for a year. He had apparently dated some but spent a great deal of time alone or with his two teenage grandchildren. Both were cautious with regard to getting into a serious relationship.

Emily mused about how differently she had approached her relationship with Hank as opposed to Doug. She knew Doug had swept her off her feet, and she felt her feet were firmly planted on the ground. She and Hank had taken things very slowly. Hank was not the least bit flamboyant. He was steady, calm and thoughtful. He was tall and slim with grey hair and eyes. She always felt at ease with him and never thought that what she said wasn't important to him. He made no effort to be the center of attention. He valued family time and was very accepting of Carter. He was willing to spend time with Carter and even seemed to enjoy watching the Braves games on television with him. That was more than Doug ever did. Life with Hank would be comfortable but not as exciting as it was with Doug, but look at how that had worked out! She was no longer the naive young woman she was when she met Doug. She realized that her relationship with Hank had continued to deepen and was becoming more important to her as time went on. Decisions, decisions.

Turning to her present situation, she was beginning to feel that she had to come to terms with whether to remain in the house. She did get alimony from Doug but it was going to stop next year when she turned 66. Did she really want to continue to live in such a large home? She was aware that there were many housing alternatives available. The question was what was right for her both financially and emotionally. Who could help her with this decision?

MELISSA: FACTUAL PROFILE

Age:	63
Occupation:	Homemaker
Marital Status:	Married to David, age 65
His occupation:	Senior executive for major auto company—lifetime employee
Years married:	40
Children:	Christopher, age 38, married to Jean 2 teenage daughters: Isabelle (15), Christina (13), live in Detroit area
	Matthew, age 36, partner Terry, age 34, no children, live in Seattle
	Hannah, age 34, divorced from Tim. 2 children: Tad (10) and Alexa (8), lives nearby
Siblings:	Tom, age 66, lives in Montana
Parents:	Her parents Dorothy and Elmer, in their early 80s live nearby.
	They moved to a smaller home ten years ago.
	His parents Steve and Phyllis, in their mid-80s live in Sarasota, Florida.
	Recently moved to a retirement community
Religious Counselor:	Pastor Barnes
Accountant:	Charles Whitney
Melissa's widow friend:	Angela
Sarasota Friends:	Jane and Bill Johnson
Health:	Melissa: chronic high blood pressure controlled with medication
	David: Cardiac issue, stent two years ago, doing well now.

Residence:	Rambling old house in Bloomfield Hills, Michigan, no mortgage
Investments:	David has a pension plan as well as a 401(k) plan
	David owns a whole life insurance policy
	They have some jointly held investments
Financial Lifestyle:	Somewhat frugal. Had a budget they mutually agreed on, annually reviewed and followed.

Melissa: Descriptive Character Profile

It was hard for Melissa to realize she had grandchildren. She thought she looked a lot younger than her age. She certainly had the energy of a younger person. It seemed like just yesterday that she and David had met and begun to date. Had she ever been that young? Anna, her closest friend in high school, had encouraged her to go with her to visit her brother in college. At the time it seemed so grown up. David turned out to be Anna's brother's roommate. The guys took them to see the football game that was being played that afternoon. Afterward they went to get something to eat. She'd really enjoyed the day and the atmosphere, but didn't think too much about it afterward.

It came as a surprise to her that during the Christmas break from school David called her and asked if she would like to go out to a movie with him. She said yes and so began their relationship. She couldn't believe that it had been 44 years ago. It just didn't seem possible.

David had gone to college for four years and after graduating went to work for one of the major auto companies in Detroit, where they both had grown up. During the time he was in school she had gone to the local community college. She graduated and was qualified to work as a Dental Assistant. She had no difficulty getting a job. She enjoyed the work, and in due time David had proposed and they had married.

Sometimes, she would ask herself what David had seen in her. She didn't think of herself as that smart or good looking. She was on the short side, and always had a mop of bright red unruly curls and hazel eyes. Her hair was the bane of her existence when she was in high school. She could never get it to do what was the style at the time.

After they were married, they rented an apartment for a while. They had fun furnishing it and went to many garage sales and consignment shops to find furniture and accessories. Both of their parents lived in the area, and they often went to one set of parents or the other for a Sunday dinner, or to watch a game or to celebrate a family event.

Melissa's parents had always valued their Sunday dinners. Her mother made pot roast or a roasted chicken with a vegetable and potatoes or rice. She loved to bake and they always had pie or cake for dessert. It felt somewhat formal but the young couple always enjoyed the time they spent with Melissa's parents.

David's parents were much more casual with regard to the meal itself. His mom would throw something together like hamburgers and fries or a casserole. However, the conversation was always lively and included others. Sports were always a big topic, particularly about Michigan teams. It took Melissa a little while to get used to these informal Sundays. Sometimes she would bring something she'd made for dessert. They'd always gotten along but were never close.

David was very protective of her and had been clear with her, that if they could manage it, he didn't want her to work after they had children. It seemed like a fine plan to her. She enjoyed her work, but was not overly committed to her job. They had two years together before they had children. After they had been married 18 months, she found out that she was pregnant. Their first child, Christopher, was born following an uncomplicated pregnancy. They were thrilled to be parents, but he wasn't the easiest of babies. He cried a lot and always seemed to be hungry. In those first few months, Melissa often thought she would rather be back at work.

However, after a while things got easier and before she knew it, they had their second child, Matthew. He was a much easier baby and she began to be busy with all the usual things that young mothers find themselves doing. She became part of a young mothers' play group; they alternated taking the children to one another's homes as well as parks and other activities like Gymboree. When Matthew was four, along came Hannah. It hadn't been part of their master plan to have a third child, but she was glad to have a little girl. She was grateful that David valued her role as a mother and supported her many child-related activities. She couldn't remember a time when her life hadn't been primarily focused on her children and extended family.

Melissa was proud of her children. They all had graduated from college and had good jobs. Her oldest son, Chris, was married and had two girls who were now teenagers. It didn't seem possible! They lived 30 miles away.

Matthew wasn't married but had been with his partner Terry for several years. He worked for a high-tech company in Seattle, Washington.

Hannah had been married to Tim, but unfortunately they had divorced. Tim's job required a considerable amount of traveling. When he came home from a week away he had a difficult time reentering family life. As a result, the family life increasingly seemed to revolve around Hannah and the children to the exclusion of Tim. They had agreed to separate in the best interests of all concerned and had a fairly amicable divorce. Hannah kept the children most of the time. Tim spent alternate weekends with them and took them out to dinner once a week if he was in town. Melissa knew things weren't easy for Hannah, who was trying to juggle work and the responsibilities of being a single mom. Melissa tried to help her out as much as possible.

She often handled all the transportation for Hannah's oldest child, Tad, who was a very good soccer player for a 10-year-old and was on two soccer teams. Hannah always seemed to need help. When Melissa looked at Hannah and her life, she was very thankful that she'd been able to stay at home and parent her children while they were growing up. David had been so supportive.

She knew David was looking forward to retiring now that he was 65. Was she really 63?! What seemed so difficult now was that for the first time they were in different places. From the time the children were born she'd gotten a great deal of satisfaction from doing a variety of volunteer work attached to the children's lives and other activities that interested her. Sometimes it was the children's school, sometimes their sports and sometimes her own interests. She'd always been an officer for the PTA in both the elementary and middle schools. It seemed that fewer and fewer people were willing to be involved.

In addition she volunteered at the local hospital. Since she always enjoyed classical music, she became an active member of the women's committee for the Detroit Symphony Orchestra. David had always encouraged these activities. Recently added

responsibilities with her parents' doctor visits and her grandchildren had reduced the amount of time she could spend on
these activities, which she enjoyed. Their social life revolved
around David's company and the country club where they
belonged where David played golf.

Now she and David didn't totally agree on how to move
forward into this next phase of their lives. She wanted to
downsize and move out of the rambling old house they had
lived in since Hannah was born. She wanted to find a smaller,
newer place near the grandchildren which required less maintenance. David had made it clear that now that he was retiring he didn't want to spend another cold winter in Detroit.
Ideally, he would like to move to Sarasota, near his parents,
at least in the winter months. He pointed out that there they
could take advantage of the cultural life available as well as
improve his golf handicap!

She felt so torn. How could she leave Hannah, a divorcee
with two children and all her issues and live in another state
even for part of the year? She would also miss spending time
with Chris's girls, but they didn't need her the way Hannah
did. As for Matthew, they didn't see him as often as they did
his siblings who lived nearby. And then there were her parents,
who weren't getting any younger and who were requiring more
of her time. Currently they had no interest in leaving Detroit.

Melissa knew she was fortunate that after all these years of
marriage, David was looking forward to spending time with
just her, without the constant demands of their adult children.
She wanted to spend time with him, too. She knew other
couples who didn't feel the same way. She missed their alone

time as much as he did, but she just couldn't see moving to Florida just yet. And if she was honest with herself she wasn't sure she wanted to be that close to her mother-in-law. Silly to think she felt that way after all these years of marriage! So many decisions—she felt pulled in so many directions!

Victoria: Factual Profile

Age:	69
Occupation:	Tenured college professor
Marital Status:	Single, never married
Children:	None
Siblings:	Brother: Travis age 67, lives in San Diego Married to Ilene
	Children: Trevor (27) and Tom (26)
	Sister: Winifred (Winnie) age 62, lives in San Francisco, married to Frank
	Children: Rodney (25) and Adam (23)
Parent:	Mother, Miriam, age 91, widow living in retirement home nearby, mentally alert.
Physician:	Dr. Stanley Ross
Stockbroker:	John O'Brien
Victoria's Health:	Breast cancer survivor (5 years)
Residence:	Home in Berkeley, California, no mortgage
Investments:	Inheritance from her aunt
Financial Lifestyle:	Careful with her money. Spent money on travel, education
	Didn't adhere to a budget but always seem to have enough.

Victoria: Descriptive Character Profile

Victoria stretched and ran her fingers through her hair. Another semester about to end. How many years had she been teaching history at the college level? She loved what she did and never regretted for a moment that she'd decided to be a college professor. She took pride in the number of students whose lives she felt she'd impacted in a positive way. Several had stayed in touch with her throughout the years.

Unfortunately, with only one semester of teaching ahead of her before she retired, she knew that she had to start thinking more about her life after she stopped teaching. Although she thought she was financially secure, she couldn't imagine herself not having a full teaching load. What would she do with all that free time? Much food for thought.

Victoria was the eldest of three children. She had two younger siblings—her brother, Travis, and her sister, Winnie. Both were very different from her in their growing up years. They still were. Both were married with children. She was particularly close to her sister's oldest son, Rodney. He admired her and always enjoyed the many hiking and camping trips they had taken when he was younger. She was proud and pleased that he was now in graduate school and talking about following her into academia.

Victoria was a tall, wiry woman with silver hair and deep blue eyes. Her trademark both on and off campus was dressing in long flowing skirts and wearing chunky silver jewelry with a variety of turquoise stones. She'd acquired her jewelry over a long period of time during the course of her numerous student and individual travels to Mexico and Latin America. She prided herself on staying fit. She ran, swam or walked almost every day.

Her parents worried about her when she was growing up because she was so skinny. They were constantly trying to get her to eat more and spend less time with her nose in a book or fantasizing about some faraway place she wanted to visit.

Also, she never seemed to want to spend much time with other children her age. Her brother and sister were always going somewhere with their friends, but she just wanted to hang around the house, read books and be involved in individual pursuits such as drawing. It never bothered her that she hadn't married. She'd had a couple of long-term relationships but had never seriously considered marrying. She valued her independence too much for that.

Victoria was content reading her books and finding interesting things and places to explore. She was a serious student and always did much better in school than her brother and sister. She went to a state college and after graduating went on to get her doctorate at UCLA while teaching at a high school. She majored in history with her thesis on the history of the indigenous people of Mexico. Over time she developed a group of friends who shared her interests in travel, history and outdoor activities. She'd travelled widely in Latin America and loved sharing her experiences with her students.

When she finished grading this last group of papers and entering the grades in the computer, she decided to try to organize her office a bit better. Papers were everywhere. She was feeling scattered and recognized that her thoughts were all over the place. One minute she was thinking about retirement, the next the summer. It felt odd not to be thinking about what she was going to teach in the fall. Not teaching a full load of classes as she always had done was going to require major adjustments in her life. She knew she wanted to identify a way to keep intellectually challenged but she wasn't sure where to start.

Victoria also needed to schedule her annual medical appointment with Dr Ross, her oncologist. Five years ago, she'd had a major health scare when after a routine breast exam she had been diagnosed with breast cancer—stage two. Fortunately it'd been caught at a fairly early stage. Consultations with two other oncologists, a radiologist and a breast surgeon resulted in a treatment plan consisting of radiation and chemotherapy. The treatment plan had been successful and now she was in remission. She was feeling well but her routine mammograms and annual checkup made her anxious. Nothing unusual, she thought.

She had always given some thought to moving to San Francisco but it hadn't seemed a viable option while she was still teaching. She also worried about the high cost of living there. It would be further away from the community and university life she cherished. On the other hand, the cultural life in San Francisco was rich. She had her sister and some friends there with whom she enjoyed sharing all that the city had to offer.

Back to her thoughts of imminent retirement. How would it change her life? How would she spend her time? What sort of life would she like to be able to lead? She had never been that concerned with her finances as she'd always had enough money to lead a comfortable life. After all, she only had herself to support and didn't have to worry about the expense of bringing up a family. She was beginning to realize that she needed to have a better idea of the implications of her financial situation when she retired. She understood the ramifications of her medical issues but not those of her financial health.

She was a member of a writers group at the University. She always valued spending time talking with her peers about her work. When others in the group digressed from the topic at hand and started talking about what life would be like when they retired, she couldn't understand why they were concerned. Retirement always seemed so far off that it didn't warrant her attention, but now she had no choice.

Her brother, Travis, lived in a San Diego suburb. She was in touch with him, but she found his wife difficult to be around for too long. She seemed to require the full attention of both her husband and her children. Victoria had little patience for women like that. Travis had two children, Trevor and Tom. She and her nephews shared an interest in the outdoors too. They always seemed happy to see their Aunt Victoria and encouraged her to share her experiences with them. She thought it had something to do with the fact that she was so different from their mother and didn't care if she got dirty or her clothes were wrinkled.

A few years ago, Victoria and her siblings had agreed that it was not in their widowed mother's best interest to continue living in her home alone. They had found an appropriate retirement community and worked together to get her settled in her new environment. Although her mother was mentally alert, she was having some health issues. Victoria thought she might need to be more available to her in the future.

She was closest to her sister, Winnie, who lived in San Francisco. Victoria and Winnie's husband (Frank) had always gotten along well. She thought she might really like to live in the city since she also was close to her sister's two children and celebrated the holidays with them. She always felt welcome at their home. She even thought her sister's children looked upon her as a second mother.

If Victoria was really being honest with herself, she had to recognize that she was afraid of what her life as a retiree would be. She knew when she was going to retire but always pushed off the decisions she needed to make. Until now, she was able to use her busy schedule as an excuse not to plan for the future. She took each day as it came. However, now Victoria had to make some decisions about the rest of her life. Where would she live and how would she spend her time? She realized she had to stop procrastinating. It was time to focus on what her retirement life would look like. She really needed to develop a course of action that would allow her to make decisions about her future.

CHAPTER Two

Assessing Your Financial Situation

*P*lanning for retirement is hard. Most people approaching retirement say they want to retire comfortably and make sure that their money lasts for the rest of their lives. While these goals are simple, the solutions are not. Financial planners would like to be able to tell you exactly how much you will need to retire in comfort, but the fact is retirement planning is far from an exact science because there are so many variables involved.

The process would be much easier if we knew exactly how long we were going to live after we retired and what our health situation would be during those retirement years. When you consider stock market conditions, tax law changes, rising health care costs and the rate of inflation, projecting your income sources and expenses gets more complicated every year.

Over the past century, the whole concept of retirement has radically changed. It used to be that you worked as long as you could and if you were lucky enough to live long enough to retire, a couple of years later you died.

In 1935, the year the Social Security Act was passed, the average life expectancy for a woman in the United States was 63 and for a man it was 60. According to the Social Security Administration, today women in the United States age 65 will live to age 86.5 and men to age 84. However, these numbers are just averages. It's expected one out of five women will live past age 90 and one out of ten will live past age 94. According to the latest population estimate, released July 2015, there are 77,000 centenarians. More than 80 percent are women. These statistics indicate that in most cases money has to last longer for women than for men.

Although planning for retirement is difficult, the best way to start is to figure out where you are financially. Once you have that data you can start moving forward.

THE RETIREMENT PLANNING PROCESS

The first step is to put together a balance sheet, which is simply a list of what you own and what you owe. The second step is to figure out what your potential sources of retirement income will be. The next step is to look at what your fixed and variable expenses are now and estimate what they might be in the future. After that, compare your anticipated income and expenses to see if it appears that you'll have sufficient income to meet your expenses. Even if this analysis does not come up with a positive answer, once you know the facts you can decide what adjustments you need to make—either to increase your income, reduce your expenses or both. (See end of chapter for related worksheets.)

A budget might have been an option earlier in your life but now it's a necessity, particularly if you no longer have a paycheck. If you overspend while you are working, you always have the potential to obtain more income. Once you stop working, if you overspend you'll have to start liquidating principal, which can create a downward spiral. Putting together a written budget and updating it regularly will help you manage your situation.

YOUR PERSONAL BALANCE SHEET: WHAT YOU OWN AND WHAT YOU OWE

We define "fixed assets" as those assets you own but that don't produce income, such as your primary residence, furnishings and your car (if you have one). Next you list your "liquid assets" which can produce income for you such as your personal investments and retirement accounts.

As for what you owe, this would include your mortgage and any current debts such as credit cards and car loans. It would also include any other financial obligations you might have such as funding higher education for your grandchildren for college or loaning your children money for a down payment on a house or business. When listing your mortgage, you need to note the terms. This would include the current balance due, the rate of interest you are paying and when the mortgage will be paid off.

SOURCES OF RETIREMENT INCOME

Sources of retirement income are divided into two categories—predictable income (Social Security and pensions) and variable income (personal and retirement investments and work).

PREDICTABLE RETIREMENT INCOME SOURCES

SOCIAL SECURITY INCOME

Social Security is a quagmire. If you aren't receiving Social Security income now, you have to decide at what age to apply for it. If you're married, you need to figure out how best to optimize your joint retirement income. You must have worked a total of 40 quarters to be eligible for Social Security income and your retirement benefits are averaged over your 35 highest earning years adjusted for inflation. If you only have 30 years of earnings, then five years will be entered as zeros, which will reduce the overall average.

Your first step is to go to the Social Security website (www.ssa. gov/my account.com) and create an account for yourself, so you can get a statement of your benefits. Alternatively you can call Social Security at 1-800-772-1213.

The earliest age you can receive benefits is age 62. If you start your retirement benefits at age 62, your monthly benefit amount is reduced by about 25 to 30 percent for the rest of your life as compared to the amount you would receive if you wait until you attain "full retirement age (FRA)" (see Appendix A for your FRA). If you wait until you're age 70 to collect Social Security benefits, they will be 57 percent higher than if you start taking them at age 62.

If you're collecting Social Security benefits before your FRA and continue to work, your Social Security benefits will be reduced if you earn over a certain amount. Specifically, if in 2020 you earned more than $18,240 your Social Security income would be reduced by $1 for every $2 earned above $18,240. This reduction continues until the start of the year in which you reach your FRA. For those hitting FRA in 2020, the annual exemption climbs to $48,600; at that point you would forfeit $1 for every $3 in earnings until the month you hit FRA.

Even if you continue to work after you have reached FRA, you can receive full Social Security benefits. Currently, FRA for those born between 1943 and 1954 is age 66. The FRA increases by two months for every year from 1955 to 1959. For anyone born in 1960 or after the FRA is age 67.

Since 1975, Social Security payments are subject to an annual cost of living adjustment. This means your payments could increase and have increased in every year since then except three (2009, 2010 and 2015). The longer you wait to collect Social Security income, the more monthly income you will receive (8% for each year you wait past your full retirement age). At age 70, the amount you are paid will not increase (except for annual inflation adjustments).

Be aware if you change your mind about when you start receiving Social Security income, you have 12 months from the date you filed your initial claim to pay back all prior Social Security payments and to file for increased benefits at a future date.

As stated previously, the amount of Social Security income you receive is based on the highest 35 years earnings. Therefore, if you continue to work past "full retirement age (FRA)," you might be eliminating some low income earning years when you first started working and replace them with higher paying years, so that the amount of Social Security income you're entitled to receive will increase. This is particularly true for women who dropped out of the workforce for a period of time or earned low wages in their early working years.

The decision as to when to start collecting Social Security benefits is complex. There is no right answer that easily applies to everyone. We strongly recommend you at least wait until you have reached your FRA if at all possible. If your physical health is an issue or you really need the income to cover your expenses you could start earlier. If your health is good and/or you have enough other sources of income, you should wait until age 70 to start withdrawing benefits. A married couple is likely to maximize lifetime income from Social Security if the higher earner delays until age 70 to start taking benefits. That way no matter who dies first, the survivor gets the highest possible benefit.

If you can't or don't want to work until age 70 and thus be eligible to receive maximum benefits, you might be able to supplement your retirement income by withdrawing money from your investments so you can delay receiving Social Security benefits as long as possible. You might compromise by not applying when you reach your FRA, but instead applying sometime before you reach age 70. The longer you wait the more monthly income you'll receive.

There are special rules which apply to divorcees. If you'd been married ten years or more, are currently single, and both you and your former spouse are age 62 or older, you can apply for half of your former spouse's benefit while he's still alive. This income will end if you die or remarry. If your former spouse predeceases you and you are age 60 or older, you're entitled to your ex-spouse's full benefit even if you remarry. In both cases, this assumes that his benefit is higher than what you would have received based on your own working record. (If he has remarried, his widow is also entitled to receive the full benefit!)

As you can see from the above explanation, we can't emphasize enough that you should seek expert advice to help you make the right decision for your particular circumstances. For additional on line information www.opensocialsecurity.com.

PENSIONS

If you're lucky enough to have a pension of some kind, you need to consider your options. Ask your pension plan administrator for a written estimate of your monthly pension income for the various payment options available to you as of your expected retirement date.

You're usually given a choice of receiving a lump sum (which you can take in cash or roll over into an IRA) or monthly income guaranteed for your lifetime (which will be a fixed amount and will not increase). If you take the lump sum payment in cash, it will be fully taxable to you.

If you're married and choose to receive income over your own lifetime only, you would receive the highest monthly payment and your spouse would have to sign a consent form. If instead, you specify that the payments will be for your life and for that of your surviving spouse (or another beneficiary) after your death, your beneficiary's monthly income will be reduced. Ask your pension plan administrator for exactly what you would receive if you chose: 1) a lump sum 2) lifetime income for you only or 3) lifetime income for you and your beneficiary.

Taking a lump sum would make sense if you have other assets and are willing to manage them yourself (or pay someone else to manage them). Also, if you are worried about the future solvency of your employer, you may consider taking a lump sum payout of your pension. On the other hand, a lifetime payout offers protection against market declines and you won't have to worry about outliving your money. You need to be aware if you make this choice, that pension payments are fixed and won't increase annually. If you have a retirement advisor she can provide you with projections which will assist you in making the right decision about which option is best for your own situation.

Finally, make sure you check with all your former employers to see if you have any retirement benefits you might not have realized you had.

VARIABLE RETIREMENT INCOME SOURCES

Your Retirement Accounts

Here we are referring to the accounts you've accumulated during your working years (401k, 403B, IRA etc). In most companies these employer sponsored retirement plans have replaced pension plans. When you retire, you have the choice of leaving these accounts with your employer to be managed or rolling this money into a self-directed IRA. If you're self-employed, you should clarify this matter with a financial advisor.

If you have more than one account, you need to list the current market value of each account. You may withdraw any amount of money from these accounts any time after you reach the age of 59 ½. If you take it earlier than this age, generally there is a 10 percent tax penalty. (There are exceptions to this rule.)

In the past, you were required to take your first required minimum distribution (RMD) from your IRAs by April 1st of the year after you turned 70.5. The second and all subsequent RMDs had to be taken from your IRAs by December 31st of each year. The amount of the RMD was based on the value at the end of December of the year preceding the year you turned 70.5 divided by a factor which appeared on the IRS life expectancy table. This factor, which determined how much you needed to withdraw, increased annually. There is a 50 percent penalty for noncompliance.

In December 2019 the SECURE Act was passed. This law delayed the required beginning age for your minimum distributions from your IRA from 70.5 to 72. This law affects those who turn 70.5 after 12/31/19. (See Appendix B for a chart which shows the old and the proposed new IRS withdrawal rates.)

If you own multiple IRAs you can calculate the RMD from each IRA account but you can take the total RMD from just one IRA or combination of IRAs. If you own multiple 401k(s) you must calculate and take withdrawal from each one separately. This is one reason why some people choose to roll over their 401(k) account(s) to an IRA after they retire.

Here again, as with Social Security, the longer you can wait to receive income from your retirement accounts the better. Ideally you'd wait to receive income from your retirement income accounts until you're required to do so at age 70.5. Any withdrawals you take from these accounts are taxable to you as ordinary income.

Due to the Coronavirus, all required minimum distributions were waived for the taxable year 2020.

Personal Investments
Here you would list any investments you own in your name that could provide you with retirement income.

Life Insurance
List what kind of life insurance you have (whole, term, universal), the death value as well as the cash value and the premium you are currently paying.

Annuities
In the past, you may have bought a deferred annuity, either in your name or in the name of a retirement account. Most of these are structured

so that the longer you wait to receive income from them, the higher amount you can withdraw. Some even have an additional rider that provides additional income if you need long-term care. Call the company to determine what your benefit choices are from these policies.

Paid Employment

When you retire, you may have the option of continuing to work part time. You might continue to work for your current employer, another employer or be self-employed. In some cases, you may need the income from work to cover your expenses. In other cases, you may choose to work past the age of 66 so that you can delay receiving Social Security until you are age 70 and thus receive the maximum monthly income from Social Security. Finally, you might work because you like what you do for a living, feel you're making a contribution to society, enjoy the intellectual and social stimulation it provides, or you may even have the opportunity to try something new.

Working longer has three economic benefits: It reduces the number of years you must rely on savings, allows more years of retirement account contributions and provides you with a delayed Social Security claim. Besides, it's nice to have some extra income! Of course, working longer isn't always an option. Health problems and family responsibilities may preclude this choice.

Projected Retirement Expenses

It's relatively easy to put together a balance sheet where you list what you own and what you owe. Projecting potential sources of income is not that hard either. A much more difficult task is figuring out how you spend your money. We find that people seem to fall into one of two categories—either they keep good records of what they spend or they have no idea how they spend their money nor do they really want to know.

However, if you're going to plan for a secure retirement, you have to know what it's going to cost you to live as you would like to live. You may not be clear about all the details of your future living situation, but you can begin the process by focusing on your current expenses. This would include your fixed expenses as well as your variable expenses such as clothing, food, etc. If you haven't paid attention to these expenses before, now is the time to do so. We recommend you keep a record of everything you spend for at least six months.

Once you have determined what your expenses are now, then you can better estimate your future expenses. If you plan to stop working, you would subtract work-related expenses and contributions made to retirement plans, but add projected Medicare premiums to your future expenses.

For most people, your largest living expense is your housing. This is a big topic, so we'll discuss this topic in greater detail in Chapter Seven. Right now, we'll assume that you are staying in your current residence at least for the first year, although you might be exploring your other options during that time.

FIXED EXPENSES

Fixed expenses are those which recur each month or year. They may not be the same every month but you know they will occur. These would include your mortgage or rent payment, your home equity loan (if you have one), your co-op or condo fee, utilities, auto loans, insurance premiums and taxes. If you own more than one home, that information should be listed as well. In the chart at the end of this chapter, we've listed typical fixed expenses.

VARIABLE EXPENSES

After you list your fixed predictable expenses, you should look at your variable expenses. These would include such items as: food, restaurants, clothing, entertainment, personal care, home maintenance, travel, cleaning people, medical care, dues and subscriptions, children or grandchildren's education and gifts. Entertainment costs may increase when you stop working.

TAXES

We find people are pretty good at listing their sources of income and expenses, but often forget to include their income taxes, both federal and state. In addition there are real estate, sales, vehicle and personal property taxes.

In the appendix, we've provided a tax table that shows the current income tax brackets for single, married taxpayers and head of household. In addition, most states and even counties tax your income as well. States differ as to how they tax retirement income. We recommend you look at your last year's tax return and then have a financial advisor help you estimate how the numbers might change when you retire so that you can determine what your tax bill might be.

Be aware that your Social Security income may be taxed. If your modified adjusted gross income (MAGI) plus half of your Social Security benefits plus all non-taxable interest income exceeds a certain level it will be taxed. Specifically, in 2020, if you're single, and this income is between $25,000 and $34,000, up to 50 percent will be taxed. If it's over $34,000, up to 85 percent will be taxed. For a married couple, MAGI between $32,000 and $44,000 will be taxed at up to 50 percent and over $44,000, up to 85 percent may be taxable. State income tax on Social Security income varies from state to state.

There were some notable changes for individuals made by the Tax Cuts and Jobs Act of 2017. In 2020 the standard deductions are $24,800 for couples, $12,400 for singles and $18,650 for head of households. Individuals age 65 and older get $1,650 more in deductions if they are single, and $1,300 for each partner of a married couple. These changes will mean fewer people will benefit from itemizing.

Another notable change is that whether you are single or married there's a $10,000 cap on the deduction you can take for any combination of state and local taxes. This includes residential property taxes and income or sales taxes. Note that the cap on this deduction for a married couple is $10,000 not $20,000.

On existing mortgage loans for your first and second home, interest is still deductible up to $1 million. However, on new mortgage loans, interest is deductible only on loans up to a total of $750,000. Interest on both old and new home equity loans is deductible only if used for home improvements (to buy, build or substantially improve your home).

If you don't opt to take the standard deduction, charitable contributions are still deductible as are unreimbursed medical expenses in excess of 10 percent of Adjusted Gross Income (AGI).

The federal income tax on long-term capital gains (for assets you sell which you held more than a year) is based on your adjusted gross income (AGI) and in most cases won't exceed 15 percent. In 2020, the 20 percent rate on long term capital gains starts at $441,451 AGI for singles and $496,601 for couples filing jointly. There is a 3.8 percent surtax on net investment income for singles with MAGI over $200,000 and $250,000 for married couples.

Of course, the provisions of Tax Cuts and Jobs Act of 2017 may change in the future. Currently, most provisions are projected to expire on December 31, 2025. Once you get all your information together, your financial planner or accountant can estimate what your taxes may be in the future.

UNPLANNED EXPENSES

There will always be expenses you didn't expect, both initially and later in your retirement years. One that we see quite often is requests to provide financial help to family members and/or friends. While these requests may be perfectly legitimate, you do need to weigh whether you can provide this help and if so how much you can afford to provide. Will it be a loan or an outright gift? This is difficult to do, so you may have to say no if the request will impact your own retirement plans. It is better to say no than to run out of money later in your retirement years.

CONCLUSION

As we have discussed in this chapter, we can't sufficiently emphasize that no matter how carefully you calculate your future income and expenses, it likely won't come out the way you expected. Some income won't be as high as you thought while some expenses will be higher or lower than you anticipated. This is why it is important to have a sizeable cash reserve, particularly in your first few years of retirement.

BALANCE SHEET

Fixed Assets (Current Sales Value)

Primary Residence $_____

Second Home $_____

Car(s) $_____

Collectibles $_____

Boats $_____

Liquid Assets

Personal Investments
(stocks, bonds, cash, etc.) $_____

Retirement Accounts $_____

Cash Value Life Insurance $_____

Deferred Annuities $_____

Fixed Debts

Mortgage Primary Residence $_____

Mortgage Second Home $_____

Home Equity Loan(s) $_____

Auto Loan(s) $_____

Other Debts

Credit Card Debts $_____

Other Obligations $_____

RETIREMENT INCOME SOURCES

Sources	Value	Estimated Annual Income	
		TAXABLE	NON TAXABLE
Social Security		$_____	$_____
Pension		$_____	$_____
Retirement Account	$_____	$_____	$_____
Personal Investments	$_____	$_____	$_____
Work (if applicable)		$_____	

EXPENSES

FIXED EXPENSES

	LAST 12 MONTHS	ANTICIPATED YEAR 1	ANTICIPATED YEAR 2
Mortgage (Rent)	$_____	$_____	$_____
Home Equity Loan	$_____	$_____	$_____
Co-op/Condo fee	$_____	$_____	$_____
UTILITIES			
Gas/Electric	$_____	$_____	$_____
Water	$_____	$_____	$_____
Cable/Internet	$_____	$_____	$_____
LOAN PAYMENTS			
Auto	$_____	$_____	$_____
Other	$_____	$_____	$_____
INSURANCE PREMIUMS			
Medical/dental/vision	$_____	$_____	$_____
Health Insurance/ Medicare	$_____	$_____	$_____

Assessing Your Financial Situation

	LAST 12 MONTHS	ANTICIPATED YEAR 1	ANTICIPATED YEAR 2
Medicare supplemental	$ _____	$ _____	$ _____
Life	$ _____	$ _____	$ _____
Long-term care	$ _____	$ _____	$ _____
Homeowners	$ _____	$ _____	$ _____
Auto	$ _____	$ _____	$ _____
Umbrella liability	$ _____	$ _____	$ _____
Other (flood, wind, etc.)	$ _____	$ _____	$ _____

TAXES

Real Estate	$ _____	$ _____	$ _____
Personal property	$ _____	$ _____	$ _____
Federal	$ _____	$ _____	$ _____
State	$ _____	$ _____	$ _____
County	$ _____	$ _____	$ _____

VARIABLE EXPENSES

Groceries	$ _____	$ _____	$ _____
Restaurants	$ _____	$ _____	$ _____
Clothing	$ _____	$ _____	$ _____
Cell Phone	$ _____	$ _____	$ _____
Home/Yard maintenance	$ _____	$ _____	$ _____
Home Improvements	$ _____	$ _____	$ _____
Auto maintenance/Fuel	$ _____	$ _____	$ _____
Bus/Train/Taxi, Uber etc.	$ _____	$ _____	$ _____
Parking	$ _____	$ _____	$ _____
Entertainment	$ _____	$ _____	$ _____
Hobbies	$ _____	$ _____	$ _____
Club Dues	$ _____	$ _____	$ _____

Subscriptions/Books	$_____	$_____	$_____
Vacation/travel	$_____	$_____	$_____
Domestic help	$_____	$_____	$_____
Gifts/Birthdays	$_____	$_____	$_____
Laundry/Dry Cleaning	$_____	$_____	$_____
Pharmacy	$_____	$_____	$_____
Hair/Nail Care	$_____	$_____	$_____
Pet Care	$_____	$_____	$_____
Education	$_____	$_____	$_____
Health Club	$_____	$_____	$_____
Legal fees	$_____	$_____	$_____
Accounting fees	$_____	$_____	$_____
Financial planning fees	$_____	$_____	$_____
Unreimbursed medical expenses	$_____	$_____	$_____
Charitable contributions	$_____	$_____	$_____
Support of others (children, grandchildren)	$_____	$_____	$_____

ITEMS TO CONSIDER As You Assess Your Financial Situation

- Put together a personal balance sheet of what you own and what you owe.

- Figure out your current income and expenses.

- Estimate what your income and expenses will be in the first year you are retired.

- Contact Social Security to determine potential retirement income.

- Recognize your Social Security income is based on your highest 35 years of earnings.

- Understand the full implications of retiring at age 62, your full retirement age, or age 70.

- Contact current and past employers to determine if you are entitled to pension income.

- Itemize your various retirement accounts. What kind, location, current value.

- List investments held in your name.

- Assess whether you could continue working on a part-time basis, if desired.

- List fixed and variable expenses.

- Be realistic about potential unplanned expenses involving family and/or friends.

CATHERINE CHAPTER TWO:
ASSESSING YOUR FINANCIAL SITUATION

Catherine began to work on the legal documents for Tom and Holly Turner, but her thoughts kept returning to her own situation. Now that Jordan had unexpectedly lost his job, she wasn't quite sure as to where to start given the hand they had just been dealt. She and Jordan hadn't anticipated retiring any time soon and had paid little attention to what retirement meant for them. She was comfortable helping others plan for their futures, but when it came to their own lives she wasn't that confident as to where to begin with her husband.

She realized that Jordan was still in a state of shock and dealing with issues that attach to the sudden loss of his job. He'd always loved his job and looked forward to going to work every day. She was also feeling a little ashamed of herself for not having previously given any thought to retirement given the focus of her professional life.

Jordan had provided her with the details of his severance package. It was quite generous; as it should be since he had worked for this company for all those years and hadn't been eliminated due to his performance. He would receive two years of salary, which would be paid to him monthly. This gave them some breathing room.

She recognized that there were two fundamental questions they needed to answer. The first was determining whether Jordan needed to find a job after his severance pay ended or or if he could fully retire then. The second was if he did retire completely, was retirement for her at the same time even an option?

In her heart of hearts, she knew she didn't really want to stop working and think about retirement, so what was the point of this exercise? She was too young to retire, wasn't she? They hadn't paid much attention to where they were financially because they had sufficient funds to do pretty much what they wanted to do without being concerned about a budget. She realized this casual attitude could not continue. It was essential for them to take a close look at what they had in place. It was also clear to her that she was going to be the one to put together the necessary financial information in order for them to understand their situation.

As these thoughts swirled around in her head she came to the realization that they really couldn't make any decisions about her working or not working without a thorough review of where they were financially.

Since Catherine paid the household bills, she knew what their expenses were. She looked first at their fixed expenses. They had refinanced their home five years earlier with a 30-year mortgage so they could pay cash for the beach house.

As for sources of retirement income, Catherine understood that at her age of 59, she was too young to start receiving Social Security income but since Jordan was 63, he could start receiving it now. She had read that it was advisable to wait to receive Social Security income until you were at least at full retirement age, which in Jordan's case was age 66, but she would contact the Social Security office to see how much income he would receive if he decided to take it earlier. Jordan had a 401(k) account worth $1 million and she had one worth $350,000. Their investments were worth

$750,000. These assets could provide them with additional retirement income.

Catherine thought that they would have to look at their situation in two phases. The first was the two years when Jordan was still receiving his severance pay. The second phase would be when that severance income ended, two years hence. That would mean that Jordan would be retiring at age 65. That seemed a pretty young age to retire to her, especially if she kept working until she was 70. But they had to be realistic—how easy would it be for him to find employment at that age? She supposed he might be able to work for himself as some kind of consultant. She didn't know if he even wanted to work, but would that be an option? Before this happened Catherine had planned on working until she was age 70—the age most lawyers at her firm stopped working, although they had no mandatory retirement age. After all, as a result of taking time off to take care of the children, she had practiced law for only 20 years and she wanted to continue to do so for at least another 10 years. She found the work intellectually challenging and emotionally rewarding.

They also had to consider their daughter, Amanda, who was applying to law school. Previously they'd said they could help her out with tuition, but now Catherine wasn't too sure if that was still possible.

It was now incumbent upon her to take the lead in a manner that wouldn't suggest that she viewed Jordan in a different way as a result of a circumstance over which he had no control. She would have to address the issue from the standpoint of her need to understand where they were without making him feel worse. It would be challenging.

Catherine decided that she was going to talk to him about this tonight. Postponing the inevitable was accomplishing nothing. She put on her suit jacket, squared her shoulders, turned out the lights in her office and left work for the day. Jordan had told her he would pick up Chinese food for dinner that evening, which they both enjoyed. After dinner, she was determined to introduce the topic.

EMILY CHAPTER TWO:
ASSESSING YOUR FINANCIAL SITUATION

Emily was expecting Hank to come over for a casual supper and a movie at home. It was Saturday night, and she had made a simple meal of quiche and a salad with fruit for dessert. They had begun to talk about the possibility of moving in together, but neither one was sure what that would look like. Should he move into her house? Should they find a new place together and if so, what might that be? A town house, a condo, what? The idea of having less to maintain appealed to her.

She realized she was still sorting out whether she wanted to move forward with Hank in this way. Some nights she wakened in a panic with her heart racing and her palms sweaty. What am I doing? What will come of me? Will I have enough money to live comfortably? I was never good with numbers and Doug always made the big financial decisions. I made one big mistake when I married Doug. Will I make another? When these acute feelings subsided, she would often fall back on her pillow in tears.

At other times she couldn't imagine what her life would be like without Hank. He was always so gentle with her and truly considerate. He never had to be asked to pitch in and help with something. She so appreciated his thoughtfulness and the sense of calm that Hank had brought into her life. Also, he was very good with Carter.

Carter was another piece of this puzzle. Did she feel she could insist that he find a place of his own regardless of his readiness to do so? Was she allowing him to postpone his own development by allowing him to live with her? This was a very complicated issue. She wanted Carter to feel that he was loved unconditionally and would always have a home with his mother, but she didn't want him to rely on her to the point that he didn't move forward in his own life.

She'd observed that since she had been dating Hank, Carter had allowed himself to develop a relationship with him. He'd even been brave enough to ask for Hank's help when he had some minor problem managing his money. Carter could never ask Doug for any help. In fact, his father rarely made an effort to see him, which she knew hurt Carter's feelings, and truly affected his self-esteem. Whether or not Carter lived with her full-time she did want him to know he would always have a room in her home.

Hank was very supportive of whatever she thought was best for Carter and had made it clear to her that he would honor whatever she decided regarding her son. He also told her that their decision to move in together was an opportunity to see how they did. Regardless of the outcome, he felt that they owed it to each other to give their relationship a chance.

Emily explained to Hank how nervous and anxious she was about making any big move, both emotionally and financially. She admitted to also being scared about how she would make out when she no longer received alimony from Doug, which was going to end next year.

All these thoughts didn't allow her to actually conceptualize what she would like to do about her living situation. Thinking about change had always been overwhelming for Emily. She felt she was leaning toward finding a townhouse or a condo to share with Hank. Although she loved her beautiful home, she didn't think it was a good way to begin a new relationship. She thought it would be better to have a place of their own that held no memories for either of them.

After dinner she and Hank moved to the sunroom for coffee and dessert. He reminded her that she'd told him how helpful the financial planner she'd worked with after her divorce was to her. He suggested that perhaps Emily should contact her to review her financial situation, which might make it easier for her to reach a decision about downsizing or staying where she was. He again reassured her that he was willing to move in any direction, but his preference was something new for both of them. He realized that they couldn't solve all of the emotional issues, but having a better understanding of her financial situation would be a place to start with regard to the housing issue. Although he was an accountant, Hank thought it would be better if she had advice from an objective source who wasn't personally involved.

Emily was relieved. Why hadn't she thought of going back to her advisor, Shelley? That was a great idea. She would get on it next week. First she would have to get all of her financial information together so that they could have a productive discussion. Hank knew her very well and never made her feel foolish or stupid when they discussed any issue. She did love him and his quiet ways.

She realized it had been awhile since she had taken a hard look at her finances. Since Doug's alimony more than covered her expenses, she hadn't really paid much attention to how she was spending her money. While her main concern right now was housing, she hoped that Shelley would be able to help her with retirement issues as well.

She knew that the longer she stayed in her house, the more repairs there would be and it would be more expensive to maintain. She also had to pay someone to do the yardwork. At least she could start by making a list of her current income and expenses, just as she had done prior to her divorce. When her alimony ended next year, she thought she could apply for Social Security income, but she was pretty sure the payments wouldn't be anywhere near the amount of alimony she was currently receiving. Actually, she realized that she didn't know when she would be eligible to receive Social Security income, how she would apply for it or when it would be best for her to do so in her situation. These thoughts always left her feeling inadequate and vulnerable. When would she ever feel like a grown up?!

At least she didn't have to worry about supporting her mother financially. Although her mother was 85, she still lived in her home and was active with family and friends and she was pursuing numerous interests. Although they had never discussed finances, it appeared her mother had enough income to maintain her lifestyle. Since Emily was an only child, she realized that she might inherit something from her mother, but she couldn't count on anything from that source for now, nor did she want to do so!

She realized that Hank, as an accountant, could probably be of tremendous help, but both of them were sensitive to the fact that she needed to address these issues with an objective party. Maybe there would come a day when they could work on matters of this nature together but they weren't there yet.

MELISSA CHAPTER TWO:
ASSESSING YOUR FINANCIAL SITUATION

Melissa pulled up outside of Tad's middle school to pick him up and take him to his soccer practice. While she waited for Tad to come out, her thoughts ran in multiple directions. How would Hannah manage everything that was on her plate if she and David relocated at this point in time?

Melissa realized that she and David were about to embark on a new chapter in their lives. She also recognized that she would miss the time she was able to spend with both of her grandchildren if she only saw them once every few months. She loved hearing about their school assignments, sports, and planned activities with their friends. She also knew they counted on her.

On the other hand, David had always been so understanding and good to her. How could she tell him she wasn't yet ready to relocate so that he could be out of the cold Michigan winter and all they had to do to survive the winters? The one thing she believed they did agree on was downsizing. She just had not gotten up the nerve to tell David she wanted to start the process in Michigan.

What about her parents? They counted on her to drive them to their various medical and dental appointments. How would they manage if she was not there and how would she tell them about this potential move? They would never tell her not to go, but they would be very upset and in some ways lost.

She truly loved David and had always dreamt of being able to spend more time with him when he retired, sharing things they both enjoyed. She just wasn't ready for it to have occurred this soon. How had these years crept up on her? It had always seemed so far off.

Her mind kept wandering from one scenario to another. She was shocked out of her reverie when Tad came bouncing into the car dragging his soccer gear and anxious to tell her about his school day. She truly would miss these times she shared with her grandchildren.

After she dropped him off at the soccer field and reminded him that she would be picking him up in about an hour and a half, she just sat in the car for a while with her head in her hands. She recognized that she needed help in sorting this all through before she could have any productive conversations with David. How could she talk to him about any of this if she was so conflicted and confused herself? Sometimes she found herself crying without knowing exactly why. She didn't want to be walking around feeling sad all the time. She was upset with herself but couldn't talk herself out of it. She was a mess and knew it. She wondered if she was truly depressed?

What were the priorities? If she couldn't figure this out on her own she really needed to get some help, but she wasn't sure where to turn. She didn't want to burden her parents or any of her children, particularly Hannah. Sometimes she felt like she was going crazy. This should be a happy time in their lives. After all, they had prepared for this and managed their finances so that when they retired, they would be able to enjoy life and not worry about money.

She also didn't want to get into any of this with her friends since she believed they would give her different opinions and advice based on their own individual situations. What to do? Tears formed in her eyes. As she sat there she remembered that she had told Hannah she would pick up something for the children's dinner that night. She roused herself and decided to drive to the deli to get them the subs she knew they loved.

As she drove, she passed Saint Luke's Church. She loved its tall spire and the way the light hit the stained glass windows at sunset. Saint Luke's was the church she and David had attended since they moved into their current house. "Hmm," she thought. "I know whom to turn to—Pastor Barnes." He was always kind and most appreciative of anything she did for the church. He wasn't young, but he wasn't elderly either. She thought he might be the perfect person to help her sort through all these issues. She made the decision to call the church in the morning and set up an appointment. She hoped this was a good place to start.

Melissa knew that David had been preparing for retirement for at least five years. In this past year, they both had attended the retirement lectures offered by his company, which they found very helpful with regard to financial matters. She knew he had a good handle on their financial situation. According to David's calculations which he had checked with their accountant, they appeared financially in good shape and well prepared for an extended, comfortable retirement. However she wondered if these calculations considered their housing situation. If they downsized here in the Detroit area, could they afford a second home in Florida or should they rent? She wished she had accepted David's earlier suggestions that she become more involved in these financial conversations with their accountant so she had a better grasp of their situation.

Victoria Chapter Two:
Assessing Your Financial Situation

As Victoria padded into her sunny kitchen to brew her morning cup of coffee and drink her orange juice, it was clear to her that she had to approach this phase of life in the way she'd approached other decisions. Knowledge had always been her ally, and she had utilized that when making decisions that she believed were right for her in the past.

She had made the decision to focus on her retirement life planning after her appointment with Dr Ross, her oncologist, which was scheduled for next week. It was important to her to know where she stood health wise as she moved into her active retirement planning.

Well, she did not have to make any immediate decisions but she could get started. Where to start? Lists. She was very comfortable making lists of things and it seemed that this might stand her in good stead now. It seemed appropriate to make two lists. The first would include where she was financially, and the other would focus on where she was emotionally.

Victoria first looked at her sources of retirement income. She was grateful that she had contributed the maximum she could over the years to her retirement plan, which was matched in part by the university. When she was younger, she hadn't given this much thought but now recognized just how important it was, as she considered what she would like to do in her retirement.

Even though she was eligible to apply for Social Security income she hadn't done so yet because she really didn't need the money. The retirement counselor at the university had told her that since she was going to turn age 70 soon, she should apply for it now, as there was no advantage in waiting past that age. She had contacted the Social Security Administration recently to determine how much income she was eligible to receive. She was pleased to learn that this income would increase annually with the cost of living.

A couple of years ago she had inherited some money from her aunt. In all honesty she hadn't paid much attention to it. She had left it with the same broker who had handled her aunt's account. The broker there assured her it was invested conservatively in "blue chip" stocks, so she had let him keep managing it. Looking at her most recent statement she was pleasantly surprised to see it was worth almost $500,000 and was paying about $10,000 (2 percent) in annual income.

As for her expenses, she had lived in the same house in Berkeley for the past 30 years, and the mortgage was paid off. She was so busy teaching that she knew she hadn't kept up with home improvements like she should have. When estimating her projected expenses she should look at all that. Should she redo the kitchen, the bathrooms? Looking around, she had to admit her home, as much as she loved it, it looked dated. On the other hand, she had toyed with the idea of selling this house and moving to San Francisco to be closer to her sister and all that the city had to offer—although she really did love her home.

Since she had lived alone for so many years and paid all the bills, she knew what her current expenses were. In the past, her major discretionary expense was travel, and she didn't expect that to change. In fact, this expense might well increase now that she could travel at any time of the year.

CHAPTER THREE

Emotional And Social Issues

Envisioning Your Future Life Style

*I*t's here—this first stage of your active retirement. Ready or not, you've arrived at this next chapter of your life. Undoubtedly, you're unsure of what to do next. Don't be too hard on yourself. This is the beginning of a new phase of life with many exciting options to explore.

Whenever we cross a new life threshold it involves change. Change is always bittersweet and often leads to feelings of uncertainty and stress. Just as you might have been feeling when you graduated from high school, perhaps entered college, started your first job, so too now you have mixed feelings. Some common ones are: Am I ready for this next step? Will I be successful? What does this mean in terms of my life? Will I make a mistake? What if I fail? Ready or not, you've arrived at this very exciting next chapter of your life.

How To Spend Your Time

Depending on your physical health as well as your emotional and financial needs, you can begin to chart your course through the sometimes turbulent waters of this new chapter in your life. Whatever you're feeling, recognize that you're not alone. Thousands of other women are experiencing similar roller coaster emotions. However, you have many options available to you. Family activities, travel, physical exercise and intellectual pursuits long postponed can all be considered without any feelings of guilt. What is key is to keep an open mind. Don't worry about failure or whether your action is right or wrong. It's okay to try something and change your mind if it turns out to be not all you expected it to be. Baby steps are fine. There's no rush. You have the rest of your life to work this out.

Contemplating how you're going to spend your time may seem daunting to some while welcomed by others. Some may feel that they have too many choices and don't know how to prioritize all that's before them. Others may feel that they are looking down a deep hole with no way out. Even though you may have postponed thinking about what you're going to do with your newfound unstructured time, now is the time for you to formulate an initial plan. If you feel so shut down that this is truly too much for you to address, we recommend you consider seeking some professional help so that you can embrace this time in your life in a positive way.

Being in limbo, regardless of the reason, frequently leads to feelings of anxiety. Many "supposed to be's" may be experienced. What is wrong with me? I am supposed to be happy. What is wrong with me? I don't know what I should be doing or feeling. What is wrong with me? I don't want to do anything but I also don't want to do nothing. Where do I fit? Do I fit? Is this all there is to life?

So many emotions potentially crashing down with no life line readily identifiable.

A New Day! Where To Start?

No matter what you envisioned, these first few weeks and months of retirement are going to require some adjustment. After a lifetime of having to be at a given place at a given time, it may be a shock to your system to not have to do so. Even if you were excitedly looking forward to your retirement this may still be a shock. This is particularly true for someone, you or your partner, who has had a demanding job or career as well as other time-consuming commitments. Truly, accepting that you don't have a daily agenda controlled by others is a major change. The need to adjust to this situation may come as somewhat of a surprise. If experienced, these feelings are well within the norm and should abate as time goes on.

The first day of this new life may feel strange and scary, but hopefully it won't feel that way for long. For starters, you don't have to give up everything you've done before. We'd encourage you to seek a balance between that which you've been doing and something new. Even if you've postponed thinking about what you're going to do with your newfound unstructured time now is the time to move forward. Remember, it's not carved in stone.

In all geographic areas, you can find innumerable activities often available to seniors at a discount. Now you have the luxury to select something based not just on the hour of the day it's offered, but based on its level of interest to you. Perhaps you've always wanted to volunteer at a museum, historic site, homeless shelter or theater, to name but a few. Now is the time to investigate these opportunities and give some thought to allowing yourself to get involved.

You may find yourself juggling feelings of being put out to pasture and not being a productive member of society with feelings of relief related to no longer being trapped by the demands of daily life that included work and other responsibilities. Rather than allowing yourself to get bogged down by these feelings look ahead if you can to today's options. You may find technology to be a helpful resource when trying to assess the choices ahead. As you know, you can find almost any kind of information online. First and foremost, think about things that you enjoy doing without feeling guilty about the fact that you now have time to do them.

Recognizing how you function best will also be a help in deciding your next steps. If you're an individual who needs structure in order to feel secure, losing the structure provided by the outside world might be very unsettling. You might have felt secure when life was predictable and not up to you to develop. If so, you're capable of putting in place a structure that will work for you. For example, if getting up at the same time every day makes you feel better about yourself by all means continue to do so!

Charting your course so that you include activities to look forward to as well as ones to stimulate your mind tends to result in a more satisfied retirement life. Finding a new way to create a balance among the various aspects of your life is key. Socializing with family and friends, expanding old interests, developing new interests, remaining physically and mentally active are all important components of life in retirement just as it has been in your life to date.

Taking Time To Smell The Roses

While we've encouraged you to find things to do in retirement that you didn't have time to do in your earlier adult life we would be remiss if we didn't emphasize the value of taking time to just do nothing. This might be the first time in your life that you have that luxury. There is nothing wrong with just enjoying the moment. You can take time to read a book from cover to cover or sit by yourself on a park bench watching the world go by or simply enjoying a sunrise or sunset. However, it's important that you don't take it too far and become isolated. Studies indicate socialization is key to a fulfilled retirement life.

If you're in a committed relationship, you may ask yourself if it's good or bad to want to do something your partner is not enthusiastic about doing. How much togetherness is desirable and good for the relationship? If you've been together for a long time, but aren't happy in the relationship, should you stay with the person out of habit or the fear of being alone, emotionally or financially? This is a good time to look at the individual in terms of the impact he or she might have on the quality of life you aspire to in your retirement years. Food for thought. After all, looking ahead to a potential thirty years of retirement together can be daunting, but we also know that it's scary to leave a familiar situation. While not advocating that you select a given course of action, it's worth mentioning that the current divorce rate in couples age 50 and over is higher than for any other segment of the population. This is known as the "gray" divorce.

Spending Time With Family

If your children and grandchildren live nearby, you may be in a position to spend more time with them in activities previously unavailable. We caution you that your time with the grandchildren shouldn't be limited to driving them to their activities but rather hopefully doing something more meaningful, interesting and mutually rewarding. You may already be helping out your children, but you should be the one to make the determination as to how much additional responsibility you'll assume when you retire.

When you are fully retired, many of you may find that you play a greater role in transporting family members to and from medical appointments. This type of activity is a component of family life but shouldn't dominate how you spend your time. Don't feel guilty if you want to say "no" to a given request. You're entitled to a life of your own. This is a difficult concept for some to embrace after having had a different role in the past.

Travel

Many women cite travel as one of the major activities they look forward to when they retire. This is the time for them to realize their lifelong dreams with regard to traveling outside of their designated vacation weeks. Travel is a broad category. All sorts of activities fall under this heading. There is something for everyone who is interested in travel. There are short-term trips and much longer ones. There are trips for neophytes and experienced travelers. Some are focused on learning while others are focused on a sport or just relaxing. Others are physically demanding, requiring considerable planning, preparation and training. There are trips utilizing all means of transportation. There are auto, bus and train trips as well as various types of cruises. There are trips to provide humanitarian services to people in need in other countries. There are group trips and those you can take on your own. You may choose to do your own research or consult a travel specialist. You can find the right trip for you to take if you're so inclined.

If you and your partner have always looked forward to planning a relatively long trip together, we would recommend you start now.

If you haven't already done so, put together a "bucket list" of all the places where you want to go. You should give priority to those trips that will be more physically demanding. As you age, you may be less able to take such trips. You also need to consider how travel expenses fit into your budget. You don't want to overdo and wear yourself out, but if you're interested in traveling we'd encourage you to do it sooner rather than later. Make every effort to travel while you're in good health and can enjoy it to the fullest.

RISK TOLERANCE

As with many other things, risk tolerance is both an emotional and financial matter. Emotionally, you may be someone who isn't comfortable taking much risk at all or at the other end of the spectrum you like taking risk. Most people fall somewhere in the middle. However, as you approach this time in your life when you no longer have money coming in on a regular basis and have to rely on income from your retirement accounts you may feel much less willing to take risks that will impact your finances.

To compound the issue further, you may have a different risk tolerance than your partner. Without sounding sexist, if your partner is male, research suggests he is more comfortable taking risks than you are likely to be as a woman. While this might have been alright when you were still making money, taking high risks when you are retired can have disastrous financial consequences, which you can't afford when you're unable to replace what you might have lost.

It's normal for you to be feeling anxious as you adjust to this major milestone in your life where your daily needs are met by withdrawing money from existing accounts as opposed to adding money on a predictable basis. You're now faced with removing dollars from accounts that up until now had been reserved for retirement. Frequently this shift results in your feeling vulnerable and concerned about taking risks. Will you be able to maintain your lifestyle, not only now but for the rest of your life?

There are two basic questions to ask yourself: 1) How much risk can you afford to take? 2) How much risk are you willing to take? Don't panic! Give yourself time to process the changes in your life. Again, while you're dealing with these concrete issues, there're a host of emotional factors also at play. This is not a simple do this or that decision. There are longstanding feelings you have about money and life. Your attitude about money in general is largely formed when you were young and how financial issues were addressed by your parents or parental figures. It's rare that you change your beliefs much in your adult life. Again, give yourself some time to process what you're feeling and know there's nothing wrong with you for having these feelings. We would be more concerned about you if you didn't experience some anxiety when faced with this dramatic adjustment in the way you receive and spend money.

Given all the changes you're facing—this is a good time for you to consult a financial advisor for a better understanding of your financial health. As you process all of what is going on in your life, you're likely to develop a more realistic understanding of your financial situation, which in time is likely to allow you to better comprehend how you're feeling about your risk tolerance in your retirement.

Differences of opinion between partners at this juncture in your lives are not limited to risk and how you deal with money. They will impact other aspects of your life as well. For instance, your partner might want to move to another location where you know no one and start a new life. That may sound just dreadful to you. Whether you and your partner agree or disagree as to the amount of risk you're willing to take or where you're going to live, now is the time you need to have an open and frank discussion with one another with regard to this critical aspect of your life. Again, if you're at an impasse, we suggest you seek the services of an appropriate mental health professional to help you with these decisions as a couple.

SOCIALIZATION

In general, socialization is important to your wellbeing at all stages of life. Women often wonder how retirement will affect their existing social circle. Now that you have more free time, this aspect of your life may become even more important.

Friends usually come from various sectors of your life. Some are work related, some are sports related, some are couple related if you're part of a couple. Some are the result of organizations to which you may belong, some may be the result of associations you've formed over the years with the parents of your children's friends. Still others may be due to joint activities such as tennis or bridge or the gym.

Regardless of how solid the friendship has been, you may experience some anxiety as to whether or not you'll still be welcomed as you were in the past. You might be concerned about your acceptance in the group. Maybe you're worried now that you're retired that the group will feel you have less to contribute. Will my friends look at me differently now that I am no longer working? may be part of your thought process. If you're not the first one to retire within your group, this may be of less concern.

In our experience, it's rare for you to lose solid friendships in retirement. It's likely that as you engage in new activities, you'll meet new people with whom you may enjoy spending time participating in both new and long-standing interests. At the same time, you may find some of your former friendships may not endure and that's OK. It's not healthy just to focus on the past. Allow yourself to embrace new opportunities and new friendships while maintaining what's important to you. One woman with whom we spoke actually became a tournament bridge player after she retired although she'd never played any card games prior to retirement.

Spirituality And Religion

As you age, you may feel an increased desire to be connected to a higher power in whatever way feels meaningful and helpful to you. Only you can assess the importance of faith and religion in your life.

Some of you may have been raised in a specific religion and have stayed involved. If so, it's likely that you'll continue to participate as you have in the past and now that you have more free time you may explore how to become more active. Most organized religions offer a variety of activities to its members in addition to the weekly religious services. These include bible study and discussion groups, as well as volunteering to help less fortunate people. These activities can provide you with an opportunity to meet other members of the congregation resulting in new friendships.

Others of you may have moved away from the religious roots of your formative years during your adult life. Now you may choose to reconsider your involvement in this aspect of your life and reengage. At this time you can decide whether to maintain your involvement with your previous religious denomination or to explore something different.

If you haven't had an affiliation with an organized religious group. You now might want to learn more about different religious philosophies. You could explore your options by taking a class offered by a community college or university in your area. Or you might attend services of different religious organizations to see what appeals to you. This may be something you and your partner have always wanted to do together or it may be something you're interested in doing on your own. If that's the case, feel comfortable meeting your own need.

As you move toward the final chapter of your life, spirituality and religion may become more important to you. If so, it's important to explore this area to your own satisfaction. However the journey turns out it will be well worth the time you have put in to the exploration. In all likelihood you'll feel better about where you find yourself at this point in your life.

*C*ONCLUSION

Accepting where you are and how you got there is important. This is the first generation where many women's lives have been shaped by their career choices. In retirement as well, you're doing groundbreaking work. The key is to identify what might be right for you at what should be an exciting time in your life. Looking ahead, maintaining an active lifestyle, pursuing interests both old and new and making time for family and friends lead to a fulfilling retirement life.

Emotional And Social Issues As You Envision Your Future Lifestyle

- Don't rush into anything. Take time to assess your options.

- Enjoy the time you spend with your family, but don't let feelings of obligation control what you do to the exclusion of other activities.

- When deciding how to spend your time, allow yourself to focus on more than one activity.

- Think before you commit. Don't feel as if you have to fill every moment of your day.

- If travel is important to you, make a list, prioritize it and make it a reality.

- Identify your comfort level with regard to risk tolerance, and make new plans with that in mind.

- When one door closes, another opens. Make room for friendships, both old and new.

- Consider the importance of religion in your life.

Catherine Chapter Three:
Emotional And Social

Catherine was pleased with the follow up meeting she'd had with Tom and Holly Turner. They'd reviewed the drafts she sent to them and made only a few minor changes. They seemed enthusiastic about getting their estate plan in order; now if only she could get Jordan into a similar mindset about his future. Although not quite the same as estate planning, it would allow him to look ahead to retirement not as an end but rather the beginning of a new chapter in their lives. She hoped he would allow himself to embrace the process of planning for their retirement.

At this point she didn't know if they needed to consult a financial planner, an accountant or both, but she knew they couldn't do anything until she put together a list of their current income and expenses. Once she figured out what these were now and when Jordan's severance package ended they would be in a better position to assess how best to proceed. After dinner, they cleaned up the kitchen together as they usually did and went into the family room to watch TV or talk.

She really did love Jordan and the time they spent together. However, she wasn't going to allow herself to get distracted tonight. She needed to start the ball rolling with regard to their future financial situation. She introduced the topic by sharing with Jordan her meeting with the Turners and how receptive they'd been to the estate plan she'd prepared for them. She told Jordan that talking to them had made her realize how out of touch she and Jordan were with their own financial situation and that they needed to do something about it.

She told him that she had taken the initiative here and started to put together their financial spread sheet. So far, it included their current incomes and the details of Jordan's severance package as well as other anticipated expenses such as Amanda's law school tuition. Once she put together all of this data, she wanted Jordan to review it to see if she'd covered everything he thought they needed to know. She was confident that it would help them to have a better understanding of the financial realities of their current life.

To Catherine's surprise, Jordan didn't get upset with her or apologize to her for the situation in which they now found themselves. He sat for a few minutes saying nothing and then said that he thought that it was a good idea since neither of them had paid attention to their spending habits in the past. Perhaps the shock was beginning to wear off. He even thanked her for being willing to put their financial information together so they could review it. He went on to say that he was proud of her for taking the first step with him. Well, he said, what a long way you've come from that frustrated girl in the law library all those many years ago. She smiled but didn't allow herself to get sidetracked into walking down memory lane. Instead she proceeded with what they had been discussing.

While Jordan had a good severance package, she had to admit to herself that she was worried about what he was going to do all day to occupy his time when, as of next week, he would no longer have a full-time job. This was going to be quite an adjustment for him, particularly since he had been used to working 24/7, but maybe it would be good for him to hang around the house watching TV or playing games on the computer for a short period of time. Jordan had loved what he did in his professional life. He truly believed that in his work he was contributing to the firm and its endeavors. In fact, the owner of the company had told him one of the reasons that his severance package was so generous was because they had valued his work so highly.

Although Jordan had always enjoyed his work she knew he had always wanted to find a way to give back to society in general. Maybe she could help him tap into his desire to make a contribution to others but in a different kind of work. She found herself enthusiastic about the potential for new opportunities for him but knew that such thinking was premature. First things first—and that was figuring out the financial piece.

Catherine was also concerned about Jordan becoming isolated and therefore remaining depressed. Most of his friends were still working, and he didn't have any real hobbies other than that he used to enjoy playing golf. She really did need to find a way to expand his social contacts without his realizing it. When they had first bought the house, he'd expressed an interest in gardening, but it had never materialized into any actual gardening projects on his part. Maybe that was something that he might choose to pursue now. The garden would certainly benefit, but then again, that was an individual pursuit, not involving other people.

Catherine viewed she and her husband as conservative spenders and not big risk takers. They hadn't taken the kids on any extravagant trips or made any outrageous purchases. It wasn't their habit to make a financial decision based on their incomes. Instead, they thought "we're both working and we love the beach so it's the right time for us to consider buying a second home." At this point, they would have to pay more attention to their financial situation particularly since Jordan didn't have a predictable income after the next two years.

They'd always enjoyed talking about trips they wanted to take some time in the future when they both were retired. However, she hoped Jordan wouldn't want to revisit these talks at the moment. She continued to envision them traveling—just not now.

One thing she was going to encourage him to do once he was no longer going to work on a daily basis was spending more time with his dad. New Jersey wasn't that far away and it would be good for both father and son. They were fortunate that his dad was currently healthy and independent but he was 92, a widower and living alone. She wondered how long that could continue.

Emily Chapter Three:
Emotional And Social

Emily hadn't seen Shelley in so many years. She wondered how Shelley would view her today. She didn't think of herself as the scared rabbit who initially had consulted Shelley when Doug had told her he wanted a divorce. She hoped Shelley would think that she'd grown, was now more together and approaching her current situation in a mature way. At least she thought she was doing just that with regard to her finances but emotionally—that was a different matter!

She called Shelley's office on Monday and was surprised when Renee, the receptionist who'd been there when she worked with Shelley before, answered the phone. They shared some pleasantries each remembering the other with warm feelings. Emily explained to Renee that she wanted to set up an appointment with Shelley to discuss moving forward in her current situation since her alimony would end next year. She asked Renee to have Shelley contact her and explain what papers to bring so that Shelley could give her the most appropriate advice.

She told Renee that she wasn't the basket case who'd originally come to Shelley for advice but that she still was prone to allowing her emotions to take over when it came to decision making and she didn't want to do that now. She assured her that she was beyond being the woman who hadn't worked in years and had no idea of how to move forward as a single mom. She told her that she had a new man in her life but was still living in the marital home. One of the items she wanted to discuss with Shelley was whether or not it would be financially preferable for her to stay in the marital home.

She made an appointment for Friday afternoon and was assured that Shelley would email her which documents she wanted her to bring with her when she came for the appointment. It was amazing how much better she felt as a result of just making the appointment with Shelley. She felt so comfortable with the idea of consulting with her again. She'd have to share with Hank how she'd felt the first time she had met with Shelley in contrast to where she was now.

When she was thinking clearly and not struggling with her emotions and fears, Emily recognized just how far she'd come since Doug had left her. Back then she'd been devastated. She'd thought she would never get over his ending the marriage but now she realized she'd been able to go on with her life and would continue to do so. She still believed that if Doug had been willing to go to counseling that maybe they would still be married. When she had initially seen Shelley, she'd felt paralyzed and like she was facing an abyss. Increasingly now she was aware of just how far she had come. She was very mindful of how gratifying her relationship with Hank had become. He listened to her and valued what she had to say in ways Doug never did. Was she actually a grown up now? It felt like it and she liked it most of the time.

She went to her computer and began to put together a list of the documents that she thought Shelley would want her to bring to their meeting. Some things she knew were important, like her most recent tax return, but she wasn't so sure about everything else. She wanted to share with Hank what she'd been feeling today as a result of her actually having gone ahead and begun the process with Shelley. It was clear to Emily that she was now truly ready to move ahead. Realizing how important it was to her to share these thoughts and feelings with Hank reinforced for her that he was an essential part of her life and one she didn't want to lose. She just needed to trust herself more and not become overwhelmed by feelings of regret and failure.

Emily always had female friends, but some were particularly important to her. Shortly after Carter had been diagnosed with ADHD, she had become part of an ADHD support group for parents. At the time, Carter was only about 6 years old. Doug never went with her, always offering some excuse. She and the women in that group had remained friends. That was almost 30 years ago. They always appreciated each other's support.

It was important to Emily to make a difference in people's lives, which is why she'd decided to work for a nonprofit when she returned to the workforce. Recently, one of the board members had asked her if she was thinking about retiring any time soon. She didn't believe that they were trying to edge her out, but she had to admit it was a legitimate question based on her age. She also recognized that she didn't feel as passionately about the work as she had once felt, although she was still totally committed to the mission. Perhaps it was time for someone younger to take over.

The thought of not working full time was appealing. However, she did want to work in some capacity. Having a sense of purpose was very important to her. Once she had a better understanding about the realities of her financial situation, she and Hank had to have a serious talk about finances. She thought to herself what a different woman she was today in contrast to where she was when Doug swept her off her feet.

She recognized that she needed to understand the risks she was facing as she moved forward with Hank. As a couple they needed to think about how best to blend their families. Harvey, his son and grandchildren (Tracey and Olivia) had been very accepting of her. The same was true of her children and grandchildren liking Hank. However, they needed to discuss how they wanted to handle holidays and frequency of contact. Lots to discuss!

Melissa Chapter Three:
Emotional And Social

As promised, she returned to the soccer field to pick up Tad and bring him home, along with the sub sandwiches she had bought for their dinner. As soon as he got in the car, he went on and on about all the good and bad things that occurred in soccer practice. Hannah thought that Tad was more verbal than most of the boys his age, and Melisa was grateful that he always seemed to enjoy talking to her.

Hannah and Tad's sister, Alexa, were already home when Melissa and Tad arrived. She stayed for a few minutes before departing for her own home and David. She was feeling better about things for the first time in a long time. She was sure David would have started dinner as she'd requested, because he knew that she had committed to taking Tad to soccer practice and picking him up. She greeted him warmly and gave him an extra tight hug, so tight so that he queried what it was for, but seemed happy to be the recipient just the same. The remainder of the evening was pleasant with the usual catching up on each other's day. She realized that she was feeling calmer although she wasn't sure why. It felt good just the same.

She didn't tell David about her decision to contact Pastor Barnes about her struggles with the implications of his upcoming retirement. She would talk to him about all of this when she had something more concrete to share and could do so without falling apart and feeling guilty. As she got ready for bed, she began to think about how best to present her feelings and concerns to Pastor Barnes.

Almost as soon as David was out the door to go to work the next morning she called the church. The receptionist wasn't even in yet but she left a message and asked for a return call to set up an appointment to meet with Pastor Barnes as soon as his calendar would allow for a non-crisis situation.

Before noon the receptionist called back and said Pastor Barnes did have time to see her on Thursday at 11:00 a.m. if that would work for her. Melissa said that that was fine and that she would be there. The receptionist asked if she could tell Pastor Barnes what her visit was about or if she preferred to tell him all about it when she got there. She paused for a moment and then said, "Oh, that's all right, I'll tell him all about it when I see him."

After she hung up, she wondered if Pastor Barnes would think someone was seriously ill or that she and David were having marital problems. She chuckled to herself and wondered how many parishioners, if any, had come to him with a dilemma such as hers. Oh well. That was what the clergy were supposed to be there for—helping members of the congregation regardless of the issue.

On Thursday morning she finished the breakfast dishes quickly so that she could make some notes for herself. She wanted to present her feelings and concerns to Pastor Barnes in a cohesive way without sounding like a whining child. She'd already decided that she would wear her lightweight pale blue dress with the white collar and cuffs to the meeting as she thought it made her look efficient, yet feminine. The right touch—she had decided—for a discussion.

She sat down at her computer and began putting together her list for their meeting. The three main issues were Hannah's situation, her parents and downsizing and how she felt about the time she spent with them as well as her competing feelings for David and wanting to spend more time with him.

She realized that she got a great deal of satisfaction out of the time she spent with both her daughter and her family and her parents. Although she would miss her longtime friends if they moved away, she didn't think she would experience the same sense of loss she believed she would experience if she was away from her family. Sometimes she thought it wasn't fair that she had to stop her routine because her husband was retiring. Expressions like "it's a man's world" often came to mind now. Why couldn't she be the one to decide on next steps? Sometimes she even had some feelings of resentment toward David. She knew she was being ridiculous, because without David's work and encouragement she couldn't have lived the life she had enjoyed. Nevertheless, she couldn't stop these negative thoughts from creeping in and upsetting her.

Also, not to be overlooked was thinking about how much work would be involved in getting their house ready for sale. Although they agreed on downsizing they would have to find a smaller place and then begin the process of combing through the accumulated possessions and memories of 40 years of life together. Daunting!

Melissa knew herself well enough to know that she'd never liked change and now she was faced with major changes. She knew David really wanted to get out of the bitterly cold winters they'd endured all these years. Was that going to mean that he wanted to live in Florida full time, part time, or what? Where would he want to live? Close to his parents for sure but in what? A house? A condo? Rent or buy? Her head was swimming. She didn't know if she could manage two homes at the same time. She didn't think David had any idea of what was involved.

All of these potential changes were stressful. She didn't like to take chances. The unknown always felt scary. Melissa truly hoped that Pastor Barnes could help her look at all of her conflicting emotions in some organized way so that she could develop some sort of plan that she then could discuss with David in a productive way. She printed her notes and put them in her purse. Tossing her coat over her shoulders she left the house and got into her car.

VICTORIA CHAPTER THREE:
EMOTIONAL AND SOCIAL

Victoria was trying to envision what life might be like without being on the university campus on a regular basis this fall and not having the responsibility for any classes. Life seemed to have sped by without her realizing it. So many mixed emotions!

She was feeling adrift and it felt uncomfortable. She didn't think she was depressed but was feeling somewhat anxious. She needed to develop a plan to help her move forward in this new phase of life. While her physical condition was monitored on a regular basis, her financial life wasn't. What she was going to do with the rest of her life seemed to be floating out there someplace.

Being a positive person, at least that is the way she saw herself, she thought she should start her list with something positive. She would write down all the things she enjoyed doing. For now it did not matter whether or not the items she listed were feasible, just what she found satisfying.

Next, she would make a list of all the things she wanted to avoid or not have to deal with in the future. This list would contain activities, people, places, etc. Her living situation might go on both lists because of her mixed feelings about the potential move.

Gathering information was also important to her. She would make a list of the resources available that might be helpful to her as she began to plan her active retirement. There were all sorts of books on this topic, but she would have to narrow her search to include those that she felt would most likely apply to her personal circumstances as a single woman.

Recently she had read "What Color is Your Parachute for Retirement?" by Nelson and Bolles and found it to be thought provoking. She'd often recommended their earlier book "What Color is Your Parachute?" to her students as they grappled with what they wanted to do, career-wise. Maybe she should take the questionnaire that was included in their retirement book.

Finally, she thought, it might be a good idea to discuss with some of her retired colleagues what they had done with regard to activities undertaken in this phase of their lives. This seemed like a project she could get into with some enthusiasm as opposed to dread. Serious attention to retirement planning was going to start after her doctor's appointment, but she could initiate this process today.

She was beginning to feel that there might be some excitement in thinking about how she would spend her time without having to think about actually earning money. What a new concept for her. She'd leave decision making on hold until she understood her physical situation better.

CHAPTER FOUR

Physical And Mental Health

*W*hether or not your impending retirement has been thrust upon you unexpectedly or it has been an anticipated event, it's extremely important that at this point you evaluate both your physical and mental health. In order to make informed decisions with regard to future plans you need to assess where you are, health-wise.

Many of the decisions you're going to make as you move forward into your retirement years will be based on the state of your physical and mental health. As we know, the aging process involves deteriorating health over a period of years. This varies from individual to individual and is dependent on many factors. One of the benefits of being retired is that you do have more time to take care of yourself. Exercising regularly and watching what you eat and drink can benefit you physically and mentally.

Physical Health

It's essential you're aware of both your current health status and insurance coverage as you consider what may and may not be viable relative to your health when contemplating next steps. Your health and health care have both financial and personal ramifications when contemplating your future life.

Health Insurance

For those of you who have an existing relationship with a primary care physician, now is a good time for you to schedule an appointment with her to discuss the frequency of anticipated medical visits as well as potential insurance coverage.

For those of you who don't fall into this category, we would encourage you to locate an appropriate primary care physician. Your existing insurance company will be able to provide you with a list of preferred physicians in your geographic area that your insurance covers. This is a good place to start your search as are the recommendations of friends.

Medicare

When you turn 65, you have seven months to enroll in Medicare (the three months before your birth month, your birth month, and three months after) or face a lifetime late enrollment penalty, (unless you're still working and have employer coverage). We recommend you sign up for it as soon as you can. That way you'll receive the benefits as soon as you are eligible. If you signed up for Social Security before age 65, you'll be automatically enrolled in Medicare Parts A and B.

Even if you keep working, when you turn 65, you should sign up for Medicare Part A since it is free. However, if you continue to work past age 65 and have adequate health insurance coverage, you may want to wait to enroll in Part B. If you decide to wait until your group coverage ends to enroll in Medicare part A and/or Part B, you'll have an eight-month Special Enrollment Period to sign up for Medicare that starts once you stop working or your group coverage ends (whichever happens first). You can also enroll in Medicare at any time that you are still working and have employer-based coverage.

If you choose to continue your existing insurance with your employer after you stop working (COBRA), don't wait until your coverage ends to sign up for Medicare. If you delay enrolling in Medicare part A and/or Part B after your Special Enrollment Period ends, you'll have to wait until the next General Enrollment Period (January 1 to March 31 every year) to enroll, and you may have to pay a late-enrollment penalty. Medicare premium surcharges are based on your income as reflected on your tax return two years prior. If your taxable income declines when you retire you need to notify them to reduce your premium accordingly.

Medicare Part A (hospital insurance) helps cover inpatient care in hospitals, skilled nursing facilities, hospice and home health care.

Part B (medical insurance) provided by Medicare helps cover doctor services, outpatient care, preventive services to maintain health and durable medical equipment. Monthly premiums for Part B depend on your income (in 2020, they ranged from a low of $144.60 to $491.60 per person.)

Medicare Supplement (Medigap) Plans offered by private insurance companies cover some or all of the costs that aren't covered by Parts A and B. Generally they don't cover long-term care, vision or dental care, hearing aids, eyeglasses or private-duty nursing. You have six months after enrolling in Part B to decide which Medigap insurance policy you should buy. This is called the Medigap Open Enrollment

Period. During this time period, insurance companies can't turn you down for pre-existing conditions. After the six months, you can still buy a supplemental policy but you aren't guaranteed to get it. Certain treatments may not be covered, prices may be higher, or insurers can decline to cover you. There are up to 10 different types of Medigap plans (depending on your state). (See "Choosing a Medigap Policy" at Medicare.gov.)

Part D plans, offered by Medicare-approved private insurance companies help cover the cost of prescription drugs. All Part D plans must meet a federal standard, but the plans available to you depend on the state in which you live. Don't make the mistake of thinking you don't need the coverage because you don't take any physician-prescribed medications. Enrollment in Part D is optional, but as is the case with Medicare Part B, if you don't enroll when you first become eligible, you may owe a penalty if you enroll later. You should review this coverage annually during the open enrollment period in the fall (October 15—December 7). Different companies provide different reimbursements for different drugs and these may change annually. In 2020, monthly premiums ranged from $12.20 to $76.40 per person.

You will be charged monthly for parts B and D. If you're receiving Social Security income, these premiums are deducted from that income. If not, you'll be billed monthly. The higher your income is, the higher amount you'll be charged for Medicare Part B each month.

Medicare Advantage Plans, often called Part C, offered by private insurance companies approved by Medicare, take the place of Part A, Part B and Part D. Sometimes these plans offer prescription coverage, as well as dental and vision care. Generally, they are less expensive than other coverage, but participants are more restricted in the choice of doctors and hospitals they can use.

Before your eyes glaze over, you're able to obtain professional advice for this decision and we recommend you do so. There are Medicare experts capable of explaining the options available to you and which one is most likely to meet your needs. Medicare.gov offers "Getting Started with Medicare" or you can call 1-800-633-4227. AARP.org/health/medicare-qu-tool offers a Medicare Question and Answer tool. State Health Insurance Assistance Plan (SHIP) helps you locate the agency in your state which provides free consultations (www.shiptacenter.org/800-633-4227)

Long-Term Care Insurance

There's a good possibility you may need long-term health care. According to the US Department of Health & Human Services (October 2017), those turning age 65 today have almost a 70 percent chance of needing some form of long-term care. According to the same source, women need health care longer (3.7 years) versus men (2.2 years). One third may never need it but 20 percent will need it longer than 5 years. It's crucial to note that Medicare won't cover these costs.

The key question is how long will you need coverage? As stated above, the average nursing home stay is 2.2 to 3.7 years, but often that's after four to five years of diminished capability and needing help at home. In 2019, the national median for a private room in a nursing home was $8,517 per month and $4,051 in an assisted living facility. Home health care averages 44 hours a week and costs $4,385 per month. Costs vary by geographic area. (Source: Genworth).

If you already have long-term care insurance, we recommend you keep it. If the premiums increase, they're still lower than what you'd pay if you had to take it out now. If companies raise the premiums, they usually offer some alternatives to keep the premiums more afford-able, like eliminating the inflation factor or reducing the length of the coverage.

If you don't have long-term care insurance, find out if you qualify for this important coverage at a reasonable price. The younger you are when you take out the insurance, the lower the cost. Often, premi-ums are reduced if both members of a couple take out the insurance. Unfortunately, since statistically women live longer than men, the cost for long-term care insurance is higher for women than men who are the same age. All or part of long-term care insurance premiums may be tax deductible as a medical expense according to your age.

When buying a policy, key factors to consider are: 1) how long you wait before you receive benefits; (typically 90 days) 2) what is the daily benefit amount; 3) the presence of an inflation factor that keeps benefits rising annually; 4) if there is a limit to how long you receive benefits (three years is a popular choice); and 5) whether home health care is covered.

If you're concerned about the cost of the long-term health care insurance policy, there are alternatives. One hybrid policy combines long-term-care coverage with a life insurance benefit or annuity. Typically, this kind of policy requires a large upfront premium. However, these alternatives are complex, so we strongly recommend you consult a financial advisor or insurance agent so that you fully understand your options before making a decision. Whatever you do, don't dismiss the need for long-term care insurance based on cost. Not having this coverage can wreck your carefully constructed budget.

Once you obtain coverage, make sure to keep your policy in a safe place and notify your family where it is kept so they can contact the insurance company on your behalf if necessary.

Other Health Care Factors To Consider

Health care needs are an important component of your life plan particularly as you move forward into your retirement years. You need to think about the availability and quality of health care wherever you live. Is it adequate for your needs? How close are you to a hospital should you need one? Are you satisfied with your current treating physicians? Do you need to find new physicians where you presently reside? If you are considering relocating, what health care will be available to you in the new location? How good are home health care options? Are any of your current physicians ready to retire? If so, seek out younger physicians who can take care of you as you age.

Exercise And Eating Habits

At this time in your life, it's necessary to take a hard look at what you need to do to maintain a healthy lifestyle. In this category, we're focusing on your exercise routine or lack thereof and your diet. It's rare that you can go a day without hearing about some exercise regimen that is good for heart health. Suggested regimens run the gamut from strenuous routines to those that are less demanding such as walking. We recommend you discuss with your primary care physician what type of regimen would be best for you based on your age and physical condition. Can you imagine what our forefathers would think if they came back to life and saw the number of fitness facilities that are present in almost every geographic location with the assortment of machines and classes designed to help keep all of us in shape?

Given that your life will soon no longer be dictated by your work or previous schedule, it's a good idea to pay better attention to your eating habits. Do you snack all day? Do you make it a point to eat breakfast? Do you find yourself drinking more alcoholic beverages? Do you have dinner early or late? How many meals do you skip in a day or grab on the run? How much fast food do you eat? Do you tend to try one diet fad after another or experience major weight fluctuations?

If you already have to follow a specific diet, then by all means continue to do so. If your eating habits are erratic, now is an excellent time to look at these habits and think about change. After all, when you retire, you don't have to get to work at a specific time in the morning. Now you're in a position to make some positive changes. We can't stress enough, there's no one right choice. It's what's right for you.

Clearly, if you have suffered from food allergies, you're already monitoring what you eat. It might also be a good idea to review them with your physician. You may develop a sensitivity to a food you were previously not allergic to and might also find out that you're no longer allergic to a food you believed you were allergic to throughout your life.

You may have a friend who raves about a particular diet she has embraced. Resist joining her until you've done your own exploration as to what is best for you to maintain your own health. The key in most of these areas is to obtain as much information as you can in order to make a decision that's right for you.

MENTAL HEALTH

Many work environments have a stated retirement age which enables you to plan for this event. However, sometimes the choice of when to retire is not yours, because your company is bought out, merged or reorganized. It may also be the result of a personal health issue that now prevents you from working outside the home. Or it may be a health issue of a family member or friend who requires your help. In these circumstances you're forced to focus on retirement earlier than you expected to do so.

Media would have you believe that you'll be happy when you retire. Think of all those pictures of smiling couples strolling down the beach together hand in hand! After all, the theory is you no longer are tied to a routine dictated by someone else. However, this isn't necessarily the case. Some people have a tough time adjusting to this new freedom after a lifetime of having to meet certain deadlines. This is normal, because you are transitioning from a structured life to one which is not. This change is bound to be unsettling.

All your life you've been looking forward to a future goal. You graduated from school, took a job, hopefully advanced in the job, bought your first house, maybe got married, may have had children, seen them through school and helped establish them, then helped with the grandchildren if you have them. Now there are no more external requirements or expectations. You've reached the ultimate goal of not having an imposed schedule or responsibility. The theory is you should be happy!

Many retirees go through an initial phase where they find it's a relief not to have to get up at a certain time in the morning, battle the commute to work and work all day. In most cases this routine provided you with a sense of purpose and a built-in support group. Without a sense of purpose, some retirees become more preoccupied with their own physical and mental health. In fact, depression and/or anxiety as opposed to elation, is often an accompanying emotion, as women not ready for retirement are forced to pay attention to this next phase of life. Loss, regardless of its cause, can result in feelings of grief.

Some of you may be experiencing uncertainty and concern about what you will do with your newfound unscheduled time. Others of you may have planned what you initially will do and thereafter. Still others may be experiencing a good deal of anxiety about being with their partner in ways that haven't been the case for years. Commonly posed questions are: "How much togetherness is expected of me? Will my partner be dependent on me for companionship? I want to continue to do or begin to do activities on my own."

Don't dwell on the "what ifs." Adopt a wait-and-see attitude. If possible, preplan some activities. Once retired, if you find you're having trouble moving forward in a healthy way, you can seek professional help to navigate these choppy waters.

IMPORTANT ITEMS TO CONSIDER REGARDING PHYSICAL AND MENTAL HEALTH

- Consult a primary care physician for a complete physical exam.

- Do the same with eye doctor, dentist and dermatologist.

- Evaluate availability and quality of health care where you live.

- Developing good eating and exercise practices are critical to your well-being.

- Register for Medicare in the seven-month window around age 65.

- Buy Medigap insurance policy within six months after enrolling in Part B.

- Enroll in Part D plans in a timely fashion to cover prescription costs.

- Consider buying long-term care insurance.

- Consult a mental health professional should you need help adjusting to retirement.

CATHERINE CHAPTER FOUR:
PHYSICAL AND MENTAL HEALTH

Catherine was feeling very satisfied about her conversation with Jordan regarding their finances. She felt they'd made a good start. While this was encouraging relative to their financial situation, she wondered how Jordan's retirement was going to impact their lives if she continued to work and he didn't.

She had read that regular physical activity actually could improve one's mental attitude. It could relieve stress, so this might be something that would benefit Jordan's mental state as well as his overall health. It wouldn't hurt her either to have some kind of regular exercise program.

Earlier in their marriage, when they had more free time, they'd enjoyed playing golf together but they hadn't done much golfing in years. The talk shows she sometimes listened to all suggested that it was important for people in retirement to be engaged in life. She recently had researched the topic online and now knew that there was a scientific reason for the need to be physically active. As she understood it, when one exercises, the body releases chemicals called endorphins. These endorphins interact with receptors in the brain, which, among other things, trigger positive feelings. This in turn reduces feelings of depression. If Jordan continued to be depressed, she feared he wouldn't do much of anything. She thought that she would need to keep a close eye on him.

She knew physical activity was something that would be beneficial to both of them. She'd maintained her figure over the years by watching what she ate but had never really gotten into exercise. Neither had Jordan. About the most she ever did was go for a walk and there was no regularity to that. She'd been really fortunate that she had lost her pregnancy weight very easily. As a result of that and the fact that she never had weight issues, she hadn't paid attention to a routine exercise regimen. A physical activity they could do together would help both of them physically and emotionally.

Jordan still played golf occasionally. She didn't think she would tell him right now, but she noticed that he'd put on a few pounds in recent years. She did love his somewhat rounder tummy, but exercise would improve Jordan's mental state and losing weight might help his self-image.

There were many fitness centers in their area. Catherine decided to find out what these places offered. Going to a fitness club would be something they could do together even if she was still working. Although she usually got to work early, she knew that her partners wouldn't have a problem if she modified her schedule one or two days a week. After all, she was a partner and that carried with it some privileges.

Health insurance for Jordan was another issue that needed to be explored. Based on the plan her firm had offered her when she returned to work, they'd made the decision to maintain individual policies at their workplaces. Catherine had checked with the human resources person at her firm and found that Jordan could have health insurance as her dependent until he reached age 65 and was eligible for Medicare. That was truly a relief. His firm had offered to carry him on their policy for a period of time, but wouldn't pay any part of the premium, so it would be more cost effective to add him to her coverage.

This would allow them to use their current physicians with whom there were very satisfied.

About three years earlier, her law firm had offered management, staff and family members long-term care insurance coverage and both of them had signed up for that. There was a premium discount when a couple signed up versus Catherine signing up by herself, even though she was younger than Jordan. So they took advantage of this price break and purchased the long-term care insurance. She was really glad they had taken care of this.

Emily Chapter Four:
Physical And Mental Health

Emily was comfortable with her decision to live with Hank. Meeting with Shelley had worked out well. It actually felt good to have a plan in mind for her future.

Shelley had explained to her that although Emily was currently covered by her employer for health insurance since she would turn 65 in three months, she should apply now for Medicare Part A, which covers hospital insurance and wouldn't cost anything. She might also want to apply for Medicare Part B as well, because it wasn't clear how much longer she would continue in her present job.

They discussed long-term care insurance, which Emily didn't have. Shelley pointed out that taking out coverage at her age was more expensive than if she had taken it out when she was younger. Still, she thought it would be a good idea that Emily have some coverage especially since she was single. However, she could reduce the annual premium somewhat by agreeing to a longer waiting period (90 days or more) and limiting coverage to three years rather than a longer period of time. Shelley also said that since health costs increase annually she recommended adding an annual inflation feature to the long-term care payments Emily would receive from the insurance company. Although the coverage would be costly, Emily really thought she couldn't afford not to get it.

In addition to her health insurance situation, she thought she needed to pay more attention to her physical health. Sometimes she worried so much about Carter or another issue that she neglected to pay attention to her own health.

When she and Doug were married she had no choice but to be physically active because of their participation in the club's tennis program. They often played in tournaments and if not, she and Doug would play singles to keep up their game. She wondered if she would even remember how to serve. Friends often said she had a wicked backhand. Doug was proud of that and frequently would remind their tennis partners that they were up against a powerhouse. Gone were those days! Even if she now had the opportunity, she wasn't sure she wanted to play tennis anymore. Too many mixed feelings and memories. She did want to do something physical, but what?

Yoga had always appealed to her, but she hadn't ever gotten around to taking any classes. Perhaps, based on her age, it would be too late to start but, on the other hand, you always heard about women doing yoga into their seventies and eighties. How would she go about finding a class or place to start? Maybe she could ask a friend or check out the local fitness centers or YMCA. Both seemed to have a variety of classes. Then again, perhaps the easiest way would be to go online and see what popped up. Emily tried to envision herself going off to yoga class with her yoga mat under her arm as she had seen many women in her area do. What would that feel like? "Enough thinking," she thought. Time to get into action mode and try it.

In recent years, she had to admit she hadn't been as careful about her diet as she should have been. However, since she'd been cooking for Hank, who always watched his weight, she'd gotten better about being conscious of what they both ate and worked to prepare healthy meals for them.

Melissa Chapter Four:
Physical And Mental Health

When Melissa arrived at the church, the receptionist greeted her warmly and commented on her dress. She seemed to really like it. While it certainly didn't have anything to do with why she was at the church to see Pastor Barnes, her comments made Melissa feel good and contributed to the positive way she was feeling about her meeting with him. She didn't have to wait long. Soon Pastor Barnes greeted her and welcomed her into his study.

"I hope the family are all well," he inquired. "Oh yes," she said, "thanks for asking. I think I am here about something you may not hear about too frequently," she said, "but I find myself in a true dilemma as to what to do in the situation I find myself in at the moment." She told him that David was retiring at the end of this year. This was something they had always looked forward to his doing. She went on to explain that she and David had always worked together, both financially and with the family, but now they were in somewhat different places. For a fleeting moment, she wondered if Pastor Barnes would give her a lecture about standing by her husband's side as a good wife and doing what he wanted.

She didn't allow herself to dwell on this thought. She went on with this clarification. David and she were in agreement about downsizing but weren't in agreement about where that should take place. David was truly tired of Michigan winters and wanted to relocate to Florida where his parents now lived. She, on the other hand, didn't feel comfortable moving away from both her parents and their daughter Hannah and their grandchildren.

Melissa continued to elaborate on the way she felt about being able to help Hannah out with the children. She truly enjoyed it and found it very rewarding. In addition, she knew her parents counted on her to drive them to various medical appointments. She knew, too, that her parents would never tell her that they didn't want her to move, but she realized if she relocated at this moment in time she would feel that she was abandoning them. She made sure that Pastor Barnes knew how much she wanted to spend time with her husband and didn't want to disappoint him either. As she concluded her presentation she realized that she was wringing her hands.

"Well," said Pastor Barnes when she sat back, "there's certainly a great deal on your plate. I've known you and David for many years and am confident that the two of you can work this out. Let's see," he said. "First, I think you should share the way you feel with David. I've always viewed the two of you as one of the more solid couples in my congregation. Since the both of you agree on downsizing, why don't you suggest that you begin to investigate that plan now in this area? It sounds like you aren't opposed to relocation to Florida, but aren't ready to do so at this time. What would you think about David going to Florida to see what rental properties might be available near his parents? Perhaps you could agree to rent a place in Florida for a few months as a starter and see how you both feel about it. David could spend the three worst winter months —January to March—in Florida. During that period, you could divide your time between Florida and Detroit."

"I've always found in my work at the church, that talking about feelings are a big help. People very often feel that they will be rejected or marginalized if they share a feeling that isn't popular, but I've found that families are more supportive of one another than not. This may surprise you, but I believe David will welcome the chance to hear how you're truly feeling."

"You know, some people lose sight of just how important family and longstanding friends are at the point of retirement. When you're facing life-changing experiences it's very important to be surrounded by family and friends. They provide emotional support. While you're concerned about your daughter and how she'll manage, I know you both well enough to know that you value your relationship and will find a way to stay connected. Knowing David as I do, he'll want to work with you to eventually live at least part of the year with him in Florida, but he'll also want you to be comfortable with the decision. Maybe he won't like Florida, but I doubt that will be the case. By the way, I can totally relate to his not wanting to deal with another cold winter in Michigan!"

Pastor Barnes suggested that he'd be willing to meet with both of them if she thought it would be helpful, but thought she should try and talk with David first on her own. She agreed with that plan. Now that she had expressed all of her misgivings to Pastor Barnes she felt better about talking to David on her own. It didn't seem so unmanageable now.

As she stood up to leave, Pastor Barnes thanked her for coming, adding that he wished more of his parishioners would look to him to discuss issues such as hers since he thought it was better to open up with regard to areas of conflict rather than let them fester. "Funny," she thought. She wouldn't have ever thought of her decision to talk to Pastor Barnes in those terms.

Driving home, Melissa's thoughts turned to other matters. At one of the retirement lectures she had attended with David, one of the speakers had spoken about how to apply for Medicare and Medigap insurance, and David had taken care of that. Fortunately, his retirement benefits would continue to pay her health insurance for the next two years until she reached age 65 when she would be eligible for Medicare.

Since she had watched some of the health issues her parents had encountered, she and David had signed up for long-term care insurance when they were in their mid-50s. She was so glad they did as she had become aware of the impact healthcare costs could have on their budget when they were older. Also, if they attempted to get long-term care insurance now at their ages, the premiums would be considerably higher. In fact, David wouldn't be able to get coverage due to his stent, which had been put in as a result of his cardiac issues just two years ago.

Melissa recognized David's health was an important concern for both of them. She had to admit that they would have the opportunity to pursue a healthier lifestyle in a warmer climate, particularly in the cold winter months. She could clearly see how being outdoors more appealed to David, particularly when he was no longer working and would have all this free time.

VICTORIA CHAPTER FOUR:
MENTAL AND PHYSICAL HEALTH

Victoria was relieved after her medical appointment with Dr Ross. He reported that everything looked good and all markers suggested she continued to be in remission. Basically he told her to continue doing what she was doing because it seemed to stand her in good stead. "Well," she said, "I'll do my best, but I'm getting ready to retire and that's going to be unfamiliar territory for me."

He said, "I've known you for many years, and I believe you'll begin this new phase in your life with a good attitude and bring to it many of the qualities you've found successful for yourself in the past." He said he couldn't imagine her not having a plan or a long list of activities she might like to explore. "I hope you're right," she said. "Right now, I'm feeling a little overwhelmed. One thing I'm sure of is that I'll continue to see you and the other doctors I've worked with in the past.

"If someone had told me when I was younger that when you retired there would be all these things to think about, I would have thought that something was wrong with them. Now I realize just how much is involved and that it truly provides you with opportunities you never thought possible. All these years when I was involved with my life in academia, I just thought, 'Oh well, when you retire, your life is finished.' Now it appears to be just the opposite. I have more options to consider than I had when I was working."

"Well, the next time I see you, I'll have made some decisions and will be able to share with you the conclusions I've reached and the process I used to get there. My goal is to lead a robust life both physically and mentally." "I'm sure you will," he said, "and I'll look forward to what you have to say. We all have to retire sometime and although I'm not ready to do so yet, I think as much information as you can get prior to that time, the better prepared you are to live a productive life."

Dr. Ross continued, saying, "One thing I never worry about with you is your commitment to eating well and staying physically fit. I'm not sure I've ever shared this with you, but sometimes I use you as a role model with some of my other patients because you've made exercise and eating well a priority for yourself. You know, now that you won't be working full time at the university, I wonder if you would be willing to take some time to be supportive to a patient who has recently been diagnosed with breast cancer and could benefit from some words of encouragement from a survivor."

"Well, I had never thought about doing anything like that, but I'd be more than pleased to do so if you thought I could help someone. I know all too well how overwhelming and scary the initial diagnosis can be."

"My," she thought as she left the office, "I never ever would have thought of being open to working with other breast cancer patients, but now that Dr. Ross mentioned it, I might give that idea more thought in terms of something I might like to do."

Victoria's thoughts turned to her medical insurance coverage when she retired. She had signed up for Medicare Part A when she was 65. Since she had health insurance through the University, she had not signed up for Part B and D. She needed to contact Medicare so that she'd be covered when she retired. She realized she needed to look into getting a Medigap policy as well. She had read somewhere that she had six months after enrolling in Part B to decide what kind of coverage to get, otherwise she might be turned down because of her breast cancer.

When she was in her fifties, she had attended a lecture at the University about long-term care insurance. She was so grateful she had signed up for it then. She had paid the annual premiums over the years even though they had increased somewhat a couple of times. However, given her bout with breast cancer, she realized she wouldn't have been able to get coverage if she had waited until now to apply. Even if she could have, it would have been prohibitively expensive. This was particularly important for her as a single person with no one else who could help her with these costs.

Chapter Five

Financial Considerations

*I*n chapter one, we provided you with the tools to assess your current financial situation. Now you have to figure out if your estimated income will cover your expenses. If it doesn't, you need to decide on a future course of action. You need to either increase your income, reduce your expenses or some combination of both. Your goal when you first retire is not just to break-even but have some excess income so you can accumulate enough cash reserve to provide for rising costs and unexpected expenses in the future.

For couples, it's very important that you make your retirement and spending decisions together. Each of you should make a list of what's important to your future personal happiness and then compare them. You both may have to modify your list in order to reach a joint decision that will meet both of your needs.

INFLATION RISK

In planning for the future, it's a given that most expenses will increase over the years. Even at the current moderate 3 percent rate of inflation, if your expenses remained the same as they are now (which is doubtful) you would need 50 percent more income 12 years from now to cover your expenses. Or put another way, if you need $100,000 after-tax income to cover your current expenses now, 12 years from now you'd need $150,000 to cover the same expenses. In 24 years, you'll need $200,000.

LONGEVITY RISK

Not only will costs increase over the years, since we're all living longer, your money will have to last longer. Recent reports say that at age 65, on average, men can expect to live to age 84 and women to age 86.5. One of every four 65-year-old persons today will live past age 90 and one out of 10 will live past age 95 (Source: www.ssa .gov). These figures are just averages—50 percent will live beyond these averages. In the second half of the 20th century, life expectancies grew, especially for people with education and money. This is due to the availability of antibiotics, improvements in surgical interventions and better prevention and treatment of cardiovascular and other diseases.

PREDICTABLE SOURCES OF RETIREMENT INCOME

By now you've gathered the necessary information to make decisions about when to start receiving your Social Security income. If you're eligible for pension income you know what that payment will be. In addition to income from your personal and retirement account investments you may have other sources of income.

VARIABLE SOURCES OF RETIREMENT INCOME

LIFE INSURANCE

If you own a permanent life insurance policy where you've built up cash value, you have various options to consider that might provide you with additional income. You should ask your insurance company for the following information:

1. "Please provide me with "in-force" illustrations for each policy I own."
2. "Please generate an "in-force" illustration using current assumptions."
3. "Please generate an "in-force" illustration using current assumptions to age 100."
4. "Please generate an "in-force" illustration using guaranteed crediting rates to age 100."

With this information a financial professional can help you interpret these illustrations and explain what options are available to you. Here are some of the many options that might be available to you:

1. You continue to pay the premiums on the policy and make no adjustments.
2. You withdraw the cash value in the policy. You pay no taxes on this withdrawal if you withdraw an amount equal to the amount of premiums you paid.
3. You convert your policy to "paid-up" status by not paying premiums and reducing the death benefit.

4. If your policy pays dividends, you can have them paid to you in cash.

5. You exchange your policy for a hybrid policy which blends life insurance with long-term care coverage.

6. You sell your policy to a third party for a lump sum. In this case, the buyer pays your future premiums and receives the death benefits of your policy when you die. However, the fees are high for this last option and you should be very careful before taking this step.

Before you make any changes to your insurance coverage, we strongly recommend you consult a financial expert who can help you understand all the ramifications of any choice you make.

ANNUITIES

Annuities are contracts issued by insurance companies. There are two basic types of annuities: the fixed annuity and the variable annuity. Fixed annuities pay a set rate of income for a specified period of time. Variable annuities invest in separate investment accounts. The income from this kind of annuity will vary according to how well (or poorly) these investments perform.

Payments from a fixed or variable annuity can begin when the contract is issued (an immediate annuity) or sometime in the future (a deferred annuity). You can contribute a single lump sum, or you can invest into the annuity periodically over time. The process of paying into the annuity is called the "accumulation phase." Once you begin receiving payments from the annuity, you have entered the "payout phase."

Typically with a fixed annuity you invest a lump sum and it begins paying you income right away (often called the "single premium immediate annuity" or SPIA). With this kind of annuity, there are three

116

different choices as to how long you are guaranteed by the insurance company to receive your income.

- ↘ The "life annuity" pays income for your life only.

- ↘ The "10 year certain" annuity pays income to you for at least ten years. If you die before ten years have elapsed, your heirs will receive the income for the remaining period.

- ↘ The "cash installment refund" annuity pays any remaining principal in the policy to your heirs if there is any left when you die.

Variable annuities are often deferred annuities, as you have the ability to invest your money and let it grow tax-deferred. You may have invested in this kind of annuity in the past as a way to build a supplemental retirement account. Now that you are preparing to retire, you can start receiving income from this investment or you can defer payments to a later date.

A relatively new variation on this type of annuity is called a "qualified longevity annuity contract (QLAC)." You might invest in a QLAC when you retire, but delay receiving income from it for at least ten years from that time. This way you can give the insurance company a smaller lump sum in exchange for larger monthly payments in the future. Any principal which remains when you die would go to your heirs. This way you create future income for your later retirement years, but you also reduce the time your other investments have to cover all your needs. Typically you might invest in this annuity when you first retire at age 65 and wait to receive payments until you are age 80.

Still another kind of annuity is the "charitable gift annuity" typically offered by universities or large nonprofit organizations. You donate money now, receive a current tax deduction for a portion of the donation (based on your age) and receive lifetime income (part of which isn't taxable). The older you are when you donate, the higher the income you will receive. The suggested maximum rates for these gift annuities are changed periodically by the American Council on Gift Annuities.

REVERSE MORTGAGES

If you decide you prefer to age in place and anticipate needing more retirement income, a reverse mortgage may be an option. It can provide you with additional tax-free income when you retire. A reverse mortgage is a federally backed loan that allows you to borrow against your home's equity, withdrawing cash that can help cover living expenses. You must own your home outright or have substantial equity in your home and it must be your primary residence (for six or more months per year). In 2015, nearly 40 percent of borrowers in the government's reverse mortgage program were single women.

The Home Equity Conversion Mortgage (HECM) is the most common form of reverse mortgage. These mortgages are available to homeowners age 62 or older. Unlike home equity loans, they require no monthly payments or interest payments. The amount you can borrow is based on several factors, including the value of your home, the youngest owner's age and the loan's interest rate. Regardless of the actual value of your home, the maximum allowed home value was $726,525 in 2019. Proceeds can be taken as a lump sum, monthly income for life, monthly income for a set period of time or a line of credit. The unused balance of your line of credit will be guaranteed to grow every year that you don't use it.

Once you withdraw money from the reverse mortgage, interest charges are added to the debt, which doesn't have to be paid off until the last surviving home owner dies or no longer uses the property as a primary residence. As long as the borrower keeps up with property taxes, insurance and maintenance, the lender can't call the loan and the lender can never recover more than the selling price for the home, even if the debt is larger.

However, reverse mortgages are expensive. These loans come with up-front costs and you'll have to repay the loan if you move out of your home for longer than twelve months. If you don't expect to stay in your home for your lifetime, other options might be preferable.

Prior to taking out a reverse mortgage you're required to attend a HUD approved counseling session. It's very important you understand all the ramifications of taking out a reverse mortgage before doing so.

Paid Employment

Based on a recent US Census Bureau study, 44 percent of people between the ages of 65 and 74 reported working part time. According to a study released in 2018 by Rand Corporation, leaving full-time work at a traditional retirement age and never working again isn't that common. Only 37 percent of US workers retire from a full-time job and stay retired. Meanwhile, about 14 percent retire to a part-time job. Another 17 percent quit their full time job and retire, only to return to the workforce some time later. About 20 percent of people continue to work either full time or part time, past age 70. (Source: University of Michigan's national Health and Retirement Study of 2,920 people in their mid-50s through age 71 surveyed over 14 years).

After you've estimated what your retirement income and expenses will be, then you can decide whether you need to continue to earn some money to augment your retirement income. If you're employed, one option would be to talk to your current employer about phased in retirement—still working, but for fewer hours. Some call this the "glide path" to or through full retirement. With the graying of America, employers are finding that the retiring population can offer valuable expertise. They're also willing to be flexible about the hours these employees work.

Another option would be to find employment elsewhere, either for another company or for yourself. You might decide to be a consultant working in the field where you previously worked or you might decide to do something entirely different. Working for yourself can be very appealing as you can control how much or how little you work. There are many people who can help you to establish and market your business. Service Corps of Retired Executives (SCORE) connects volunteers with small businesses seeking advice or mentorship.

Some new retirees choose to work in the nonprofit world where they may earn less but where their work usually has social impact. Facing perhaps decades in retirement, it's important for many people to make these retirement years meaningful, useful and productive.

If you're currently self-employed, you have the luxury of deciding when and how long you want to work as long as you are mentally and physically able to do so.

Extending one's working life beyond full retirement age solves several retirement problems, particularly for women. As we stated earlier, according to the 2016 US Census report, generally women earn less than men—about 81 cents on the dollar. This means not only lower lifetime income but also lower monthly Social Security benefits. As previously stated, time spent out of the workplace as a result of childbirth and caregiving shorten many women's careers. When benefits are calculated, additional years of work at higher levels of earning offset the less lucrative years or replace the non-working years that many women had earlier in their lives. If you work longer, your Social Security income might increase, and at the same time you can build up your retirement funds.

Projecting Retirement Expenses

Some retirement planners estimate that employed people will spend 70 to 85 percent of what they spent while working when they retire. The rationale for this estimate is that retirees won't have to spend money on a work wardrobe and commuting expenses, etc.

Actually, we would disagree with this approach to income needs. Instead we see expenses in retirement as taking place in three different phases. They frequently are referred to as the go-go years, the go-slow years and the no-go years! There are no given time frames for these three phases. They depend on your personal circumstances.

The first phase would be when you first retire. Particularly in your first year of retirement, you may have extra expenses. For instance, you may have wanted to redecorate your living room but never had the time to focus on it. Now you do, but it costs money. As previously discussed, another favorite expense for new retirees is travel. Instead of taking one trip a year, you may take several or a longer, more expensive one.

Typically, the go-slow years are more sedentary. Life has settled into more of an established routine. At this time your expenses may be less than in the first phase.

In the no-go years, your expenses will be more health-related. Your major expense will be paying people to help you with various tasks such as paying bills or transporting you to doctors, or providing health-related services.

Items To Consider When Making Your Financial Decisions Before You Retire

- Realize that your expenses will increase as you age.

- Understand that chances are you will live longer than you anticipate and plan accordingly.

- Review your life insurance to see if it can provide you with additional income.

- Consider various annuity investments as a way to provide reliable retirement income.

- If you take out a reverse mortgage, be sure to understand the full implications of your decision.

- Consider working for pay or volunteering.

- Look at your retirement in three phases: the go-go years, the go-slow years, the no-go years!

CATHERINE CHAPTER FIVE:
FINANCIAL CONSIDERATIONS

At this point, Jordan and Catherine had had several subsequent conversations about their financial situation. They soon realized that they needed to consult with a professional to help them sort through their options so they could make some decisions.

As part of the severance package, Jordan's firm had provided him with an opportunity to meet with both an employment counselor and a financial planner. They decided to start by meeting with Joe Schwartz, the financial planner.

When they went to Joe's office, they immediately were put at ease. His office reminded Catherine a lot of her own office. It was nicely furnished but not overdone. It had lots of windows and was on the ninth floor of a downtown office building. Catherine had visited Joe's website ahead of the meeting and was pleased to see he was a CERTIFIED FINANCIAL PLANNER™ practitioner and had been in business in downtown Washington for twenty years. She also was glad to learn he was 45 years old, younger than they were—so he could be their advisor for a long time should they choose to continue to work with him. At the same time, he was old enough to have had experience assisting other people who were in circumstances similar to theirs. He had a female business partner about his age and four staff members to assist them. She liked the fact he wasn't a sole practitioner, so if he wasn't available there would be someone else to give them advice in his absence if necessary.

Actually, she realized that their situation was somewhat unique, since they really hadn't done much planning and now were forced to make some decisions that they hadn't considered previously. Joe had sent them a questionnaire ahead of their meeting, which was somewhat similar to the one she provided to her clients for their estate plans. However, in addition to providing their basic personal information including their assets and liabilities, he also asked for their expenses. Catherine was relieved to see that the information she'd already assembled was what he needed to see. She had filled out the form and then reviewed it with Jordan so they were prepared for this meeting. They brought the questionnaire with them, together with last year's tax return. It felt good to finally be working as a unit on this aspect of their lives

Catherine had obtained their Social Security information, which in her case, was pretty depressing. She had worked 17 years as a lawyer. Previously she had worked in the summers in college and law school but never earned that much money. She was a long way from having the full 35 years of earnings required for maximum Social Security payments. Jordan was in much better shape given his salary level and the number of years he worked. In fact, he would be continuing to pay into the Social Security system from his severance pay, which would increase the number of higher paying years that Social Security used in their calculations.

Somewhat to their surprise, Joe asked them questions about their parents' health as well as their own. Again, the news was good. Her parents were in their 80s, living on their own in an apartment. Jordan's father was doing fine at age

92—although he was beginning to have balance issues. Based on their family histories, it appeared that they had many years to live. That certainly put things in perspective. If they both retired now, the money they had would have to last a long time—a sobering thought! Joe also pointed out that their costs of living would increase annually.

He asked if they anticipated receiving any inheritances from their parents. Even though Catherine was an estate planning lawyer she'd never discussed money with her parents so had no idea what their financial situation was. She knew they seemed financially comfortable and never complained about money so she assumed they were okay. In fact, she realized she didn't even know if they had wills! As for Jordan's father, in the past Jordan had gone over his father's finances. From his analysis of his father's pension and Social Security income, Jordan determined his dad had enough income to cover his expenses. However, Jordan didn't expect anything in the way of an inheritance.

Joe asked about their life insurance. They had to admit that all they had was through their firms and it was term insurance. They previously had term insurance of their own, but that just covered them until the children were through college, so the answer was no.

Next he asked questions about their work. Did Jordan intend to go back to work and if so what did he think would be a reasonable amount of money he could earn? How long did Catherine intend to work? He pointed out that the key issue was whether either one of them or both of them could stop working and still be financially secure.

Catherine suspected that from a financial point of view, they couldn't both retire. Even if she kept working, she wasn't sure whether Jordan could stop working and fully retire without their making serous adjustments to their current lifestyle. She told Joe she really liked working and would like to continue to work until she was at least age 70. She realized that they had been talking so much about Jordan's situation she hadn't actually discussed her thoughts about this with Jordan. She could see the expression of surprise on Jordan's face as she told this to Joe!

Following this meeting with Joe, it was obvious to both of them that in order to plan for their future they needed to determine what kind of employment Jordan could find and what it would pay. Therefore, the next step was to meet with the employment counselor, Judy Byrne.

Jordan made an appointment to see her the next week. At their meeting, she gave Jordan a set of tests to see what he might be best suited to do and might want to do. After all these years working for the same company, Jordan had never thought about doing anything else, but now he had some choices. In a way this was giving him an opportunity to think about his work in a different way.

The tests indicated that Jordan was good working with people and was detail oriented. Neither result was a surprise, since Jordan always got on well with the management team as well as those reporting to him at his firm. In addition, as a lawyer he had to be good at details. Judy suggested that since he did have two years severance pay that he take the next few months to investigate different areas of interest.

Since Jordan had indicated to Judy that he regretted never having much time to do any volunteer work she suggested that he find a charity he was interested in and volunteer for it. She told him most charities were always looking for people to help and since he was a lawyer, he had valuable expertise to offer. This would be a good way for him to meet people and might even possibly lead to a job opportunity.

Jordan liked this idea. He was particularly interested in volunteering with a nonprofit organization that helped disadvantaged children. Judy suggested he check into some of the local organizations to see which one might appeal to him. Catherine was encouraged to see that following these meetings Jordan was beginning to look to the future rather than dwelling on the past. Certainly, this was better than seeing him mope around the house!

Emily Chapter Five:
Financial Considerations

Emily realized she had a lot of decisions to make and was glad she had Shelley to give her financial guidance. However, it was complicated, because although these were primarily financial decisions, they were also emotional ones.

She decided to start with the financial decisions. She was almost 65 years old and making $100,000 a year at the nonprofit organization she had been with since she'd gone back to work when Carter didn't need her to be at home every day when he returned from school. She was totally committed to the mission of the nonprofit, but perhaps it was time for a change. The part of the job she particularly liked was fundraising. She wasn't quite ready to stop working full time nor was she sure she could afford to do so. Maybe she could find a part-time job as a fundraiser with another nonprofit that would pay her about half of what she currently was being paid, which would allow her to have a more flexible schedule.

As previously stated, Emily's monthly alimony payments from Doug would stop when she turned 66. At that time she would have reached what was called her Full Retirement Age (FRA) and be eligible to receive Social Security income regardless of how much she was earning. Shelley had told her to contact Social Security to determine how much income she would receive based on her own work history. She found out that it wouldn't be that much due to the fact she hadn't worked for the required 35 years and some of the time she had worked she hadn't made that much money.

However, Shelley also said that since she'd been married to Doug for over ten years and he was currently receiving Social Security income, Emily would be entitled to receive half his Social Security income as long as she didn't remarry. Doug always had earned a good living and most likely was now receiving the maximum Social Security income. Half of his Social Security income wasn't as much as her alimony income, but still was more than the Social Security income that she was entitled to receive based on her personal work history. In addition, Shelley explained to her that unlike her alimony, her Social Security income would increase annually with the cost of living.

Shelley further pointed out if Doug predeceased Emily, she would be entitled to receive half his Social Security income. However, she would have to stay single to receive this income. In sum, it would be to her economic advantage not to remarry at this time. She and Hank had had several discussions about moving in together and what that would be like, but they'd never discussed marriage. It was premature.

In addition to these sources of income, she did have her share of Doug's pension plan, now worth $750,000, as well as her own retirement account worth $250,000, for a total of $1 million in retirement funds. She wasn't required by the IRS to start taking income from these funds until she was 72 years old, but she could withdraw money from those accounts before then if she needed more income. Emily hoped she could postpone taking money from the retirement plans until she was required to do so, but it was reassuring to know she could supplement her other income from this source. By the time she turned 70, she thought she would be ready to retire completely. Her other major asset was her home, worth about $600,000, which had no mortgage.

She anticipated that in five years she would have transitioned from working full-time to part-time and ultimately, no time. When Doug had asked for the divorce and moved out of their home, her job at the nonprofit provided her with a much needed sense of self-worth. The chairman of the board consistently expressed to her how much the board appreciated all she had accomplished as executive director. She also valued her relationships with the members of her staff. They had almost become part of her family. She recognized that initially she had needed their reassurance and personal support. At this point she didn't think she still needed that any more, but was somewhat reluctant to give up that potential for support. By age 70, her life would be more settled, which would lead to greater sense of security.

After figuring out her potential sources of income, Shelley and Emily reviewed her expenses. When Emily made a list of all the expenses related to maintaining her home, she had to acknowledge that it really cost much more than she'd allowed herself to acknowledge previously. Since she'd always had sufficient funds to meet any and all expenses, she hadn't focused on them. However, she knew she could no longer ignore this financial outlay.

She also recognized that the house had sentimental value to her. It was where she had made a home for Doug and the children, raised her family and spent hours having it look just so. Like it or not, Doug was gone and the children were grown.

Now that Hank was in her life, she was ready for a change. She realized it was time to sell her house and to start a new chapter. She was fortunate to have found someone like Hank— they seemed so compatible. Life was relaxed with him and fun! From a practical point of view, if she moved in with Hank, they could share the housing costs. They'd had several discussions about where they wanted to live and whether they wanted to live in a house or an apartment. Hank had suggested they start by renting an apartment, and she thought that would be a good way for them to begin their life together. It certainly would be much less expensive than maintaining her four-bedroom house. In addition, she thought it would be better for both of them if they moved to a new place of their own with no lingering memories.

Melissa Chapter Five:
Financial Consideratons

Melissa felt much better after her conversation with Pastor Barnes. She and David usually went out for brunch together after church on Sunday. Then they went home and read the Sunday newspapers. She thought that might be a good time to talk to David about how she was feeling about the implications of his retirement. It was going to involve a lot of change for both of them.

Melissa had an established routine with her volunteer work as well as helping out Hannah and her parents. She wasn't sure how she would feel when David was home full-time. She thought of that old saying she had heard—"Marriage is for better or for worse but not for lunch." She wondered how David would occupy his time. She certainly hoped he didn't want to spend it all with her, as much as she loved him.

When they returned to their comfortable home after brunch, she asked David if they could sit down and talk about their future together. He'd always told her that they were financially well-off, but what did that mean? She asked him to go over all that with her so she had a better understanding of their situation. He'd always handled the investments and even the bill paying in their family. She needed to know more about their financial situation.

Recently, Melissa had become more aware of the need to know about one's financial situation since Angela, one of her friends from church, was widowed suddenly. Similar to Melissa, although Angela had a rough idea what her household expenses were, she hadn't been involved at all with their investments. She was devastated emotionally but also frightened as she only had the most limited knowledge of their financial assets. Melissa didn't want to be in the same situation. It was time she was better informed. David hadn't excluded her, she just never had expressed any interest in this aspect of their lives

As Pastor Barnes had predicted, David was pleased to know that she wanted to learn more about their finances. He started by telling her the sources of retirement income they would have. He was eligible for the highest level of Social Security income due to his many years of work and the level of his earnings. He explained if he applied for Social Security income next year, when he was 66, he would receive close to $2,900 monthly. However, if he waited until he was 70 years old to start collecting it, then that monthly income would increase by 132 percent, or 8 percent a year, to at least $3,800. Since he had a good pension from his company as well as other assets to provide them with income for the next four years, he thought it made sense for him to wait until he turned 70 to collect this Social Security income. Obviously, the state of his health was a factor. Although he'd had a stent put in a few years ago, his cardiologist had told him he continued to do well. He was willing to take the chance that he would live another four years to collect the higher income.

Since Melissa hadn't worked outside the home she wasn't eligible for her own Social Security income. However, she was entitled to receive half of David's Social Security income when he applied for it. If she outlived him, as statistics indicated she would, then she would receive his full Social Security income as his widow.

David's pension was $50,000 a year. He had set it up so that if he died before her, she would continue to receive this same income after he died. Unlike Social Security income, this annual income would stay at that same level and wouldn't increase with the cost of living. He explained to her that he had had the choice of taking his pension in a lump sum and rolling it over into a retirement account where he could direct the investments or receiving this annual income for the rest of their lives. After their accountant, Charles Whitney, had reviewed the numbers David had given him, he agreed that it would be better for David to take the lifetime income stream. David liked the certainty that they would receive this pension income as well as Social Security income regardless of what the stock and bond markets were doing.

In addition, David had a retirement account with his company worth $600,000, and they had $1 million in investments. Here again, he wasn't required by IRS to take income from his retirement account until he was age 72. He would like to defer taking money from this account as long as possible since that income would be taxable. From a tax point of view, if they needed to supplement their income, they would be better off taking money from their own portfolio rather than from their retirement accounts.

David had a rather large whole life insurance policy on his life that would pay Melissa $1 million when he died. Over the years, it had built up a cash value which they could tap into if necessary. At this point, he was having the cash value pay the premiums so they didn't have to pay those out of their current income.

Their house was worth about $650,000 and they had no mortgage. He had been surprised to learn in the retirement lectures he attended that many people about to retire still had a mortgage on their homes. It had been an early goal for him to make sure that it was paid off by the time he retired, and he was proud he'd been able to do that.

Even though this was a lot of information for her to absorb, Melissa felt much better now that she had a somewhat better idea of their financial situation. She was reassured to know that it appeared they could maintain their current lifestyle when they retired. However they still needed to discuss further the issue of downsizing their home in Detroit as well as the possibility relocating to Florida, for at least part of the year.

VICTORIA CHAPTER FIVE:
FINANCIAL CONSIDERATIONS

Victoria had made a list of her income sources when she retired in June. She had the retirement funds she had accumulated over the years from the university as well as her Social Security income, which she would apply for when she turned 70 in July of this year. Also, although she had never withdrawn anything from the investment account she'd inherited from her aunt, she realized she could start taking money from that account if she wanted to do so.

As for her expenses, she didn't think they would increase much from the current levels, but on the other hand she didn't think they would decrease. As she looked at her preliminary estimates of her income and expenses it appeared that she would have some extra income left over. However, she knew she would have expenses that weren't in her regular budget. For instance, there were some repairs that she really should make in the house if she decided to keep it. In fact, even if she sold it, she probably would have to make some improvements in order to get it in shape to sell. Travel had always been a passion of hers. She knew she wanted to do more of that when she retired and that would add to her expenses. In addition, she had to be realistic about rising costs of living. Expenses such as real estate taxes and utilities didn't go down, they always went up.

She started thinking about her writers group from the university. She wished she hadn't been so dismissive of their discussions about what they would do when they retired. Now she realized she should have paid more attention when they talked about these matters. She had been so busy she'd lost touch with this group but thought now would be a good time to touch base with a couple of them who had retired and ask them how they had adjusted to their new life after academia.

Although she didn't have to make a decision right away about whether to stay in her current home or move to San Francisco she realized she needed to get some more information to help her make the decision. First, she needed to stop reading the real estate ads on her computer and instead actually visit some of these apartments that were available in San Francisco. They all looked great in the pictures on the internet, would they be as good when she actually saw them? Also, she knew she would have adjustments to make if she moved to the city. Her town house was spacious and sunny, and since she was the only one living there, she had lots of space to store her belongings. If she moved to an apartment, she knew she would have to downsize in order to buy a place she could afford. Instead of having a couple of bedrooms and baths and a full basement, she probably would have to settle for a one bedroom/den in the city. Also, she would have to pay the monthly condominium fees and real estate taxes. From her preliminary research she knew real estate taxes in the city would be higher than what she paid currently.

Since her sister, Winnie, had lived in the city for awhile and knew the city much better than she did, Victoria asked her to go with her the next weekend to visit some open houses. She certainly didn't have time to get her house organized to make a move before she retired, but she did need to understand whether selling her house and buying an apartment was even possible financially when she retired.

CHAPTER SIX

Putting the Financial
Pieces Together

Various Approaches To Withdrawal Plans

By this time, you know what your predictable income sources (Social Security, pension payments, etc.) are. Now you have to decide how much income to take from your retirement accounts and personal investments and when to do so. At this stage, we strongly recommend you have a professional financial advisor help you make these decisions since there is so much for you to consider. Also understand once you put together a plan, that it isn't set in stone. You may start out with one approach but there is a high probability you will want to make adjustments to your plan as time goes on.

Ideally the combined income from your pension, Social Security and your investments should cover your annual expenses without your having to touch your principal. As a practical matter, only very wealthy people are able to do this. Instead, most people find they need to withdraw both income and principal to pay their retirement expenses.

Formulas To Simplify Withdrawal Plans

Strategies to reduce or eliminate the need to withdraw from investments when the stock market is declining is essential. This is especially true during the first few years of retirement when large losses, coupled with withdrawals, would cripple an investment portfolio and cause it to fall short of its original goals.

Over the years, financial experts have tried to develop various guidelines that show how much you can safely withdraw from your investments and be relatively certain your money will last as long as you do. Two popular withdrawal theories are the "4 percent rule" and the "bucket approach."

The so-called "4 percent rule" was developed originally in 1994 by financial planner Bill Bengen. This rule postulated that with a portfolio of 60 percent stocks and 40 percent intermediate-term bonds, you could withdraw 4 percent of your principal the first year you retire. In subsequent years you would withdraw the first year's withdrawal amount plus the inflation rate of the prior year. Based on historical data in 1994, your savings should last 30 years. If you thought you would be retired for longer than 30 years, you would withdraw a lesser amount.

For example, under this theory, if you had $1,000,000 in combined retirement and personal investments, the first year you would withdraw $40,000. Typically, you would withdraw this in monthly payments of $3333.30, but if you so desired you could withdraw it annually or quarterly. The next year, if last year's inflation rate was 3 percent, you would withdraw $41,200 ($400,000 plus 3 percent of $40,000). Each year you'd adjust your withdrawal rate based on the inflation rate the prior year.

However, keep in mind this formula was based on market performance as well as longevity in the last century. You also may need to reduce this withdrawal rate if you retire early, have a major unplanned expense or there is a stock market decline that reduces your principal.

The "bucket approach" suggests you should put aside three years' expenses in a cash or money market account. This "bucket" would also hold enough for major expenses you expect to make, such as buying a new car or travel. In your second bucket, you would hold enough money to cover your expenses for the next seven years. You would invest this sum in high quality bonds, certificates of deposit or fixed annuities. In the third bucket, you would invest the balance of your money in higher growth, long-term investments such as common stocks.

You start by paying your current expenses from the first bucket account, but replenish it annually from income and assets in the second bucket. The rationale for this "bucket" approach is that you would have sufficient cash reserves to cover your expenses if the market declines when you first retire. Having an ample cash reserve helps you to avoid panicking and liquidating all your investments at the wrong time.

Still another approach suggests that you should figure out what your fixed expenses are and from that subtract your predictable income. Then you cover the gap if there is one by buying a fixed annuity, which will provide sufficient current income to make up the difference.

The problem with these, and other formulas, is that there are always unexpected expenses which can wreak havoc with your budget. That is why it's important to have some kind of cash reserve. Whichever approach you choose, we'd suggest you have a larger cash reserve than you had during your working years (at least one year's expenses) set aside for these events. We can't overlook the fact that these decisions are impacted by your personality as it relates to your tolerance for risk. When you first retire, if you're concerned about the possibility of a market decline, you should have even a higher cash reserve of three to five years expenses. Everyone's situation is different, so as we have already suggested—having professional guidance at this time in your life is essential.

When To Receive Your Retirement Income

Most people are used to receiving a regular monthly paycheck. You can arrange to have a similar arrangement when you retire. Your Social Security and pension income will be paid to you monthly and can be paid direct to your checking account. After you have figured out what you think your monthly expenses will be, subtract this predictable income from expenses. Then you will know how much you will need to cover the rest of your expenses. Next, arrange to have this amount paid to you monthly from your retirement accounts as well as your investment accounts. If you're not sure how much to take or from which account, your financial advisor will be able to help you make these decisions.

How To Receive Your Retirement Income

We suggest that once you know how much monthly retirement income you need, that you have the income from all sources paid directly into your checking account. This way, you won't have to worry about checks getting lost or not being deposited when you're out of town.

CONSOLIDATE YOUR ACCOUNTS

Over the years, you may have set up accounts at various banks and brokerage firms. Now is a good time to consolidate these accounts. You need to keep your retirement accounts and non-retirement accounts separate from each other, but it will be easier for you to monitor your investments and your withdrawals if your investments are in one institution. We also recommend you set up monthly, quarterly and annual payments, if possible, online.

ADJUSTING YOUR EXPENSES

PAYING OFF DEBTS

If you still have a mortgage, you might consider paying it off depending on your personal situation. A number of different factors affect this decision. Paying off your mortgage is both a financial and emotional decision.

From a financial point of view, if you itemize your tax deductions, the interest you pay on your mortgage may be one of the few tax deductions you have left. In addition, the investments you would sell to raise the money to pay off your mortgage might appreciate more than the amount you're paying in interest. On the other hand, if you owe a relatively small amount on your mortgage and the interest deductions are small relative to your payment, it might be a good idea to pay off your mortgage in its entirety.

From an emotional point of view, there's no denying it's a good feeling to be debt-free when you retire. Furthermore, if you don't have this major debt, psychologically you might not worry about your investments as much when the stock market declines, as it does periodically.

If you have a current credit card balance, we would recommend you pay it off as soon as possible since the interest you pay on outstanding balances is usually high and is not deductible. Once it is paid off, we suggest you pay it all off monthly. Also, you should consider the possibility of paying off any auto loans since this interest isn't tax deductible. However, if you are paying a low interest rate (like 1 or 2 percent) you might keep it.

REDUCING OTHER EXPENSES

If you implement a less costly standard of living now, you reduce the risk of having to make a radical adjustment later in life when you're older and less able to adapt to change. For instance, if you and your partner have two cars, you may find you only need one or even none when you retire depending on where you live. Now that you have time to do so, you may cook more at home. If traveling by air, you could travel mid-week, when air fares are lower, or drive if feasible.

BUDGETING FOR MEDICAL EXPENSES

Many people overlook medical costs when planning for retirement expenses. These costs are unpredictable but can be significant. In April 2019 Fidelity Investments estimated that a couple age 65 who are both eligible for Medicare will need $285,000 for medical expenses and health care during retirement—mostly to cover Medicare and Medicare supplement premiums, plus the costs Medicare and Medigap won't cover. This doesn't include dental care, nursing home or long-term care costs. The breakdown on estimated costs is $135,000 for men and $150,000 for women (due to our expected longer life expectancy). We expect these costs will continue to rise.

CAREGIVING

Another expense many don't anticipate is caregiving. Often, people think Medicare will cover most of these costs but they don't. About

7 percent of caregivers are 75 or older, typically a woman caring for a partner or other adult relative or friend (source: 2015 report National Alliance for Caregiving and AARP Public Policy Institute).

Caregiving needs come at three levels. The first is for home services, which involves shopping, cooking, cleaning, running errands and light housekeeping. The second involves hiring someone who will help with bathing and toileting and other hands-on tasks. The third is for a licensed nurse practitioner who can handle the medical management if necessary. The cost for caregiving assistance depends on the level of care needed.

If you're retired and have more free time, you may feel that it's your duty to assume some or all of this responsibility for a family member or friend. But you need to realize that caregiving is both a monetary expense and an emotional experience. Give careful consideration as to how much time you're devoting to caregiving and don't overcommit. Be mindful of your own health. You may need to hire people to help you.

The Family Caregiver Alliance's "Family Care Navigator" helps families locate government, nonprofit and private caregiver support programs. (www.caregiver.org/family-care navigator)

LOANS AND GIFTS TO FAMILY AND FRIENDS

Another unplanned expense might be loans and gifts to family and friends. For example, your daughter and son-in-law may ask you to loan them money toward the purchase of a first home or for starting a new business. If you decide you can afford to make this loan, be sure to have a written agreement spelling out the interest rate you will charge as well as the repayment terms. This way, if the loan is not repaid, you can take the loss on your tax return.

You also may be asked to give money for something like education for your grandchildren. According to the IRS, in 2020, as an individual you can give up to $15,000 per person annually, and this income is not taxable to the recipient and is not tax deductible for you. If your spouse consents (even if it is your money), you can give an individual $30,000 annually. If the education cost is in excess of this amount, you can make the payment direct to the educational institution and in that way provide more support than the $15,000.

If you decide to make a loan or a gift, make sure you can afford to do so. Don't feel guilty if you have to say you can't grant their request. It's important that you have enough money to pay for your retirement years. You don't want your largesse to impoverish you.

CHARITABLE GIVING

For some people continuing to donate to charities when they are retired is important. Under current law, if you're itemizing tax deductions (rather than taking the standard deduction), charitable donations are still tax deductible. If you can give appreciated securities instead of cash, your cash flow is not affected as much.

Even if you don't itemize, if you're age 70.5-plus, you can transfer as much as $100,000 tax free direct from your traditional IRA to IRS approved charities each year. This "qualified charitable distribution" has the advantage of counting toward your required minimum distribution but doesn't show up in your adjusted gross income.

TAXES

It may seem obvious, but we're often surprised that people fail to include income taxes, (both federal and local), in their budget projections. Obviously, these are a key component of retirement planning. When you worked, most of your taxes were probably taken care of by your employer withholding sufficient amounts. Now you may be able to arrange for taxes to be withheld from some or all of your retirement distributions. However, you may have to supplement these payments with quarterly estimated tax payments. In any case, ask your accountant to project what your taxes will be as you enter this new chapter in your life. This is particularly important during the first few years of retirement as you adjust to receiving new sources of income.

Conclusion

Regretfully, there're no magic formulas about how much you can safely withdraw from your accounts each year. Your best strategy, particularly in your first year, is to keep track of your income and expenses as you adjust to your new life. We strongly recommend you review your income and expenses annually. Your circumstances will change, as will tax laws, stock market conditions and inflation. You will need to adjust accordingly. As always, we urge you to reach out to financial planning professionals to help you plan. Their job is to make sure you make wise decisions during your retirement years, which in some cases may last as long as you worked!

Items To Consider As You Put The Financial Pieces Together

- Set up a plan to provide sufficient income to cover your expenses.

- Be ready to adjust your plan as circumstances change.

- Maintain a large cash reserve.

- Consolidate your retirement and investment accounts.

- Arrange to have various sources of income go into your bank account.

- Have your regular expenses paid automatically from your bank account.

- Pay off your debts if possible—but seek professional advice before paying off your mortgage.

- Reduce your expenses if necessary.

- Budget for medical expenses, including Medicare.

- Be cautious about assuming caregiving responsibilities.

- Make sure you can afford to loan money to family and/or friends, which may not be repaid.

- Arrange to have sufficient income taxes withheld from your income and/or pay quarterly.

- Adjust your charitable giving if necessary.

CATHERINE CHAPTER SIX:
PUTTING THE FINANCIAL PIECES TOGETHER

Based on the information Catherine and Jordan had given to their financial planner, he'd put together a written retirement plan that included three different scenarios. He sent this report to them so they would have time to review it prior to their next meeting.

In the first scenario, he assumed that they would both retire when Jordan's severance ended in two years. At that time, Jordan would be 65 and Catherine would be 61 years old. As Catherine had suspected, this approach wasn't going to work, even if they really cut back on their lifestyle, sold the beach house and moved to a smaller home. Giving Amanda any financial aid for law school wouldn't be possible. It was obvious that even if Catherine wanted to retire in two years, this wasn't a viable option.

In the second scenario, Joe assumed Catherine continued to work until age 70, as she indicated she wanted to do, and Jordan retired completely when his severance ended when he reached age 65. In this scenario he assumed Jordan would wait one more year until he was at full retirement age (age 66) to apply for Social Security income. Joe had proposed the second scenario since they didn't know if Jordan could find work. This scenario indicated that money would be tight, but if they watched their expenses, which they never had done before, they wouldn't have to alter their lifestyle that drastically.

In the third scenario, which he called the "best case," Joe assumed Catherine continued to work until age 70 and Jordan was able to earn some money annually starting a year from now. He assumed Jordan would continue to earn that income until he was age 70, when he could apply for the maximum Social Security income. Obviously, this third scenario would allow them to build their assets further, both in the retirement accounts and in their own names.

Catherine and Jordan reviewed Joe's recommendations. At the same time they reexamined the projected expenses they'd given to Joe to see if they still seemed realistic. They also discussed whether Jordan wanted to work and if so, what he would consider doing. Jordan realized that even though he would receive severance pay for the next two years, that he probably should start investigating employment possibilities now. The older he got, the harder it would be to get back into the workforce. Although he had been resistant at first, he thought he better meet with the employment counselor his company had made available to him and see what his options were.

The following week when they met with Joe again, they went over the second and third scenarios. Joe suggested that they start using some kind of computer program that would help them track their expenses. He thought the idea of Jordan's meeting with the employment counselor sooner rather than later was important but pointed out that at least the severance pay gave them some breathing room. As for helping Amanda with law school, he suggested that they tell her at this point they couldn't do much to be of assistance and it would be a good idea for her to explore financial aid opportunities. If Jordan was able to get a job that paid enough, they might be able to help her in the future.

As part of their planning, Catherine realized she needed to have a financial talk with her parents. Once they'd learned about Jordan's situation, they had been very tactful and supportive. She needed to make sure that they were all right financially, because if they would need financial help from her and Jordan in the future that would impact their own retirement plan. She doubted her sister, Judy, (who didn't have a high paying job) could be of much help. In their family, it wasn't considered good form to talk about money, but at this point, given Jordan's situation, she thought she could introduce the topic by asking them whether their estate planning documents were up to date. After all, that would be natural for her to ask since that was her area of expertise.

As Catherine and Jordan got up to leave, they thanked Joe for all his help, which had been invaluable. His analysis helped them begin to plan for their future, but they thought they would need his financial planning advice on an ongoing basis. In addition, they really hadn't paid much attention to how their retirement plans or portfolio were invested. They no longer wanted to be so casual about these important assets.

Jordan's firm had paid for this initial retirement plan, but they understood they would have to pay for investment management in the future. Catherine and Jordan were inclined to ask Joe to do this but decided they needed to go home and talk all this over before making a decision. They were greatly relieved that they had some kind of plan to follow going forward.

Emily Chapter Six:
Putting The Financial Pieces Together

Emily was feeling better. There were a lot of decisions to make, but she was getting to the place where she could begin to do so. Although she had decided to leave her present job, she wasn't ready to submit her resignation notice just yet. She knew once she told her organization she was going to leave her position as the Executive Director, the search for her replacement would start. When that person was identified, she assumed there would be some kind of transition period.

She belonged to the local chapter of the Association of Fundraising Professionals but hadn't been very active. She thought she would attend the group's next meeting and do some networking. At the same time, although she had practical experience raising money for her nonprofit, she knew there was a formal certification program in this area. After doing some research, she found out that there was an online course she could take to obtain this credential.

Emily realized that planning for her retirement had provided her with a financial focus she hadn't had before in her life. Shelley had helped her to recognize that when she left her current job she wouldn't have to work full time but things would be tight if she had no earned income. Emotionally, she knew she wasn't ready to stop working altogether, as she liked the feeling of being productive and helping people in need achieve their goals. She would prefer to make a gradual transition from full time work over the next five years. Certainly, having a part-time job would meet her need to feel useful and give her a sense of purpose. At the same time, it would allow her to withdraw less of her retirement funds during this transition phase.

Shelley had pointed out that this money was going to have to last for her lifetime. Since her health was pretty good, that might be a long time. After all, her mother seemed to be going strong at age 85. Also, with inflation, her living costs would continue to increase.

Since Emily had decided to sell her house, she'd contacted her neighbor Amy Johnson, a realtor who specialized in selling homes in her neighborhood. Amy spent some time with her and said she thought the house was worth around $650,000. She said that it was in pretty good shape, but she would recommend repainting a couple of rooms to freshen up the look of the house. She also suggested that it would be a good idea to declutter it. If Emily was going to downsize, she would need to go through everything and see what she really wanted to take with her and what she would like to sell or donate. Amy suggested that perhaps her daughter, Jill, might want some of the furniture, but it had been her experience adult children had enough of their own and didn't want any more.

The timing of this move seemed to fit in well with the progress Carter was making. He told her that he'd appreciated her providing a roof over his head for all these years. He admitted that he'd continued to live there because it was so easy. However, recently one of his colleagues had talked to him about renting a house with a couple of other men. They would each have their own bedroom and bath but would share cooking and living facilities. Given the talks he had

had with Hank over the past few months, Carter said he was feeling comfortable about moving out on his own. He also shared with her how much he'd appreciated the time Hank had spent with him and was looking forward to expanding their relationship.

Emily was thrilled to hear this news. One of her major concerns with regard to selling the house was having to ask Carter to move out on his own before he was ready to do so, but if he thought he was ready for a new life as well, that was great. It all seemed to be falling into place. A lot of change, but exciting change!

MELISSA CHAPTER SIX:
PUTTING THE FINANCIAL PIECES TOGETHER

Melissa was pleased with the progress she and David had made planning for his retirement. After their recent discussion about finances, she had a much clearer picture of their financial situation. It seemed that they would have enough money to meet their expenses when David retired. Now she thought it was time for them to make decisions about where they were going to live.

While they'd agreed to downsize, they still hadn't decided whether they would move full time to a smaller home in the Detroit area or in Florida. Alternatively, they might compromise by buying two places. However, Melissa knew she wasn't ready to take on the responsibility of owning two places, particularly since she still was very involved with her parents and grandchildren. She had to admit she had never liked a lot of change in her life. After all, she had lived in the same neighborhood and in the same house most of her life. Her routine over the years had been pretty predictable!

In any event, they agreed to contact a realtor and discuss with her what their house was worth as well as what kind of house they might want to buy. She'd seen ads for a new group of townhouses being built near Hannah's home and not too far from their present home—some even had elevators. They didn't need an elevator now but there might be a time in the future when that would be important.

David and Melissa had continued having financial discussions on a regular basis. Since Melissa had expressed her concerns, she told David that her widowed friend Angela had no knowledge about her financial situation. In addition, she also had no idea how to get into her husband's computer. She was panicked until she discovered that he had made a list of his passwords which were in a file in his desk drawer.

Hearing this story, David said he could imagine how scary that would be for anyone. He followed up by showing Melissa his fireproof file cabinet in his home office where he kept all their records. He had a key to this cabinet, which he kept in a drawer in their bedroom. He explained that all of their financial statements were on his computer but he also had printed out copies. He put this information, as well as a current list of his passwords and the monthly statements of their investments, in a three-ring binder. Then he put the binder in a place where both of them knew where it was. Melissa thought it would be a good idea to tell Hannah and Chris where this information was kept as well.

As for the monthly bills, he had all of them on auto pay. At the same time, he showed her how he could access the monthly statement on his computer so there weren't any big surprises. He said initially he'd resisted doing this because he distrusted the internet and the lack of privacy. However, he'd discovered that it was much easier to have the basic bills paid automatically.

The following Sunday afternoon, Melissa decided to discuss with David her concerns about her parents as well as Hannah. She thought this would help him understand why she was reluctant to pull up stakes and move to Florida full- or even part-time right now. She recognized that although

Hannah had a well-paying job, it was very demanding. Her major needs weren't financial, but what Hannah needed most was her mother's help with her children. As they both knew from their own personal experiences with their family, children often need more attention in their teen years than when they are younger.

As for her parents, she wondered how much longer they could continue to live in their current home. She felt she needed to at least discuss with them the idea of their moving to a retirement home. Some of her parents' friends had already done so and seemed to be happy. She thought that it would be better for them if they moved while they were relatively healthy and could actually enjoy the many activities available to them in one of these places. In addition, it would be good to have someone else besides herself responsible for getting them to their medical appointments!

Victoria Chapter Six:
Putting The Financial Pieces Together

When Victoria walked with her fellow professors to their usual seats in this year's graduation ceremony she wondered if she would experience different emotions than she had in the past. This would be the last time she would be doing this as a full professor. Each graduation seemed special but this one more so because it was her last one. Saying goodbye to her last group of new graduates was particularly meaningful to her. As with everything it was an end and a beginning for them and for her. Well, time to turn the page and move on with her life.

Victoria's 70th birthday was June 15th. A couple of months ago she'd spoken to the Social Security office and had set the wheels in motion to start receiving her monthly Social Security income in June. She had also applied for Medicare Parts B and D. When she looked into the Medigap choices, she realized there were several different plans. However, she had spoken with Sally, one of her friends in the writers group, who was retired. Sally told her which plan she had selected and that it covered most of her medical costs. It was expensive but Sally, like Victoria, was single and she wanted to make sure these expenses were covered should she need medical attention.

The major decisions for Victoria were how much to withdraw from her retirement plan and when to start receiving the payments. She called the phone number on her retirement fund statement. The person she spoke to told her she had several choices as to how she received her distributions. Victoria also learned that the IRS required that she start receiving required minimum distributions when she turned 72. She could take this amount out all at once or arrange for monthly distributions. She further explained that since it would be taxable income to her, she could have taxes withheld from her distributions so she wouldn't be hit by a big tax bill at the end of the year.

Victoria was getting overwhelmed. Based on her age, the decision about Social Security was relatively easy to make. Now that she had to decide how much income to take from her retirement account, she realized she needed some expert advice. She had gathered the facts but she could only get so far on her own. This wasn't a time for her to try to wing it!

She decided to call John O'Brien, the stockbroker who managed her inheritance. She had only met with him in person a couple of times in the past, although she had spoken on the phone with him regularly. John told her that he'd worked with several of the professors at her university and was familiar with the retirement investments they had available to them. She thought he could be helpful to her at this point in her planning process.

She decided to make an appointment to meet with him to discuss her various retirement fund options. When they spoke on the phone prior to the scheduled meeting he'd asked her to put together some very specific information. She was pleased to realize that she had already assembled most of it, including last year's tax return.

When they met, Victoria explained that the major decision she needed to make was how much to withdraw from her retirement plan when she retired. Should she wait until she was 72 to take the minimum distribution the IRS required or should she start taking income from her retirement funds now? Should she only take out the required minimum distribution or should she take more? Should she take it annually or monthly? Should she have taxes withdrawn from the distribution and if so, how much? Should she make any changes to her investments in the plan? So many questions!

John reviewed all the information with her. He said he wanted to look at her situation more closely in order to determine which approach would be best for her. However, from the information she'd provided it appeared for now that the income from her retirement plan, the Social Security payment and the income from her investments would cover her expenses with a little left over. He recommended that she start taking the distributions from her retirement plan on a monthly basis and withhold federal and state taxes from these distributions. These distributions could be paid into her checking account each month together with her Social Security payments. Victoria liked that idea because it would be similar to what she was used to with her monthly salary checks.

So far, so good. But then Victoria told John about her dream of possibly moving to San Francisco. That obviously was going to affect this retirement plan. She shared with him her preliminary research. She'd located a couple of apartments that met her specifications but they would require her to downsize considerably. She was having second thoughts about whether the tradeoffs were worth it. She would have less space, be further away from the university and all the courses she could take when retired and she wouldn't be able to afford to travel as much as she wanted to do. John assured her that he would look at a couple of options for her. One would include a move and one would not. She thought that would be very helpful to her in making a final decision.

Part Two

Adjusting to Retirement
In the First Year

CHAPTER SEVEN

Housing

*H*ousing is one of the major expenses everyone has before and after retirement. Contemplating where you should live is often complicated because there are financial, physical and psychological considerations to be addressed. Your home creates a sense of belonging and value. Your physical environment has a lot to do with your staying healthy and independent. It's important that your living situation fits your current level of physical and mental ability. At the same time, you should look ahead to your anticipated future needs. At this stage in your life, it's likely you'll be spending more time in your home than previously.

Initially when you were facing retirement and making other important decisions, we recommended that you stay in your current home. Once you've worked your way through the first year, you can focus more easily on whether or not you want to change your current living situation. Where you live is a critical decision.

There are many factors to consider in this regard. Is the neighborhood safe? Are you near quality medical services (physicians and hospitals)? Food stores? Do you want to be in a city or in a less congested area? Are you close to family members and friends and activities you enjoy? Is public transportation and/or car services readily available?

Studies indicate that most people prefer to age in place. This may work for you, particularly during the first years after retirement. However, as you get older, you may need to revisit this decision due to your physical condition or that of your partner. Also, recognize that aging is likely to have health care implications. It's best to make plans now, not when an event has taken place that forces you to make a decision in a short time frame.

STAY IN YOUR CURRENT HOME

There are many reasons why you might decide to stay in your current home. You may want to live where you are now because you are attached to it emotionally. You like staying with the familiar, where you know your neighbors and enjoy the environment. However, other factors such as changes to the neighborhood, a sense of isolation and physical health issues might motivate you to move.

You also need to consider the costs of staying in your home. You should look at your projected expenses versus your income and determine whether you can afford to stay. Include the following in your calculations: the mortgage/home equity loan payments (if you have them), real estate taxes, condo or association fees, etc. The less obvious costs, which many don't budget for and can be considerable, are those for repairs and maintenance. A rule of thumb for annual maintenance costs for a single-family dwelling is 1 percent of the value of the home. Of course, this is dependent on the age of your home.

THE VILLAGE MOVEMENT: AGING IN PLACE

For people who want to age in place and can afford to do so, there is the village movement, which is gaining traction. A "village" is a community organized by a group of people who want to live in their own homes as they get older, with all the resources needed to live active lives. You pay an annual fee to belong to these organizations, usually located in major cities. In return for this fee, volunteers provide you with the services you may need to stay in your home. These might include courtesy rides to a medical appointment, help with a shopping trip and minor home maintenance. They also may offer social activities for the members. (www.vtvnetwork.org)

HOME SHARING

For various reasons, you may decide to share your home with another person on a permanent or temporary basis. Your motivation may be safety, companionship, additional income and/or the ability to stay in your home longer. You might rent a bedroom and bathroom to someone in exchange for rent or help with transportation and/or household chores. Typically, this person is unrelated to you, and might be the same age or younger, such as a student. Sharing your home with a stranger is obviously a very personal decision and won't work for everyone.

Another way to add to your income would be renting out living space on an occasional basis. Still another alternative is for a group of three or four friends to buy a house together and to share expenses and household duties.

If you decide to take the approach of house sharing, consult a nonprofit service or ask an eldercare professional, friends or a family member to help screen candidates. It's important to make sure your "tenant" qualifies personally and financially. A background check, a damage deposit and a written lease agreement are advisable (www. nationalsharedhousing.org).

Modifying Your Home

If you decide to stay in your home, you should consider making modifications. Even if you don't need them now, it's likely you will eventually. There are consultants who can provide you with a home safety assessment. Useful changes that can be made include sturdy grab bars in the bathroom, higher toilets, shower seats, slip resistant bathroom floors, brighter lighting, lever-style door and faucet handles. If you have stairs, you may add railings and/or a chair to take you upstairs or down. You might convert existing living space on the ground floor to accommodate a bedroom and full bath.

For more specifics, review the "aging-in-place" checklist at the National Association of Home Builders (www.nahb.org) and type "aging-in-place checklist" in the search field. This site also includes a directory of contractors who are certified aging-in-place specialists (CAPS). Another resource is "HomeFitGuide" from AARP.

Moving To Another Place In The Same Georgraphic Area

Let's say that you want to stay in your same geographic area, but are ready to downsize, or as some call it, "rightsize"—moving to a smaller living space or one where your living quarters are all on one level. If you decide to move, realize this isn't going to happen overnight. You need to allow enough time for all the pieces to fall into place, typically 12 to 18 months. If you make this decision, there are many options open to you.

One common solution is to move to an apartment. There are several different kinds of apartment houses. For instance, it might be a multiage apartment or part of a retirement community. Having someone else take care of minor repairs and accepting your mail and packages can be quite liberating! Your apartment may be closer to restaurants, entertainment, food stores and cultural pursuits. When living in an apartment, you are surrounded by other apartment dwellers, which may make you feel more secure and provide socialization.

ACTIVE ADULT LIFESTYLE COMMUNITIES

You may prefer to move to a 55-plus independent living community. Typically, these age restricted communities don't provide medical care. Usually, they will have a clubhouse where recreational and social activities take place. These communities may also offer a meal plan, housekeeping, linen service and transportation (www.seniorhomes.com).

SHARED HOUSING

This would be one house where two or more unrelated people live. Typically each resident would have their own bedroom and bathroom but have shared common living areas (www.nationalsharedhousing.org).

COHOUSING

For those who want companionship but want to maintain independence as well, there is the relatively new concept of cohousing. Multiple family residences are clustered around an open space anchored by a common house where the group meets and may eat together. As of

2017, there were 165 nationwide, with 140 in planning stages. You own your home and pay into a fund to maintain facilities. Collectively the residents decide how to use the funds. (www.cohousing.org)

CONTINUING CARE RETIREMENT COMMUNITIES (CCRC)

These residences offer a tiered approach to the aging process, accommodating residents' needs as they age. Health services, meals, personal care, housekeeping, transportation and emergency help, as well as a host of social activities are included. These different levels of care are offered in one location.

When choosing such a community, you need to determine its financial stability as well as the various payment arrangements available. Find out how the occupancy rates have changed over the past few years (Ideally you want to see a rate of 90 percent or higher.) Ask to see the community's audited financial statements for the past five years and a recent actuarial study.

When you agree to move to a CCRC you aren't making a real estate purchase but rather an agreement with the CCRC to provide service and a place to live for the rest of your life. You pay an entrance fee (which may be partially refundable to your heirs) and a monthly fee. Part of either or both of these fees may be tax deductible. To get an idea of how much annual costs might rise, ask to see the past five years of fee increases.

Most CCRCs are owned and operated by not-for-profit organizations. The different types include: (A) Extensive or Full life care, (B) Modified life care, (C) Fee for Service and (D) Rental. Type A contracts tend to have higher entry fees than others. Be aware the CCRC reserves the right to not admit you if it doesn't think you qualify physically or financially.

This approach is not inexpensive, but is appealing to many, particularly if you don't want to rely on your family and stay independent as long as possible. This option requires considerable research. It's important that you understand the terms of the contract you'll have to sign. We recommend strongly you seek legal advice before entering into this agreement because of the ramifications for your future life.

The Commission on the Accreditation of Rehabilitation Facilities International is a nonprofit group which accredits health and human resources. Go to the website (www.carf.org) and then to "resources" and "retirement living" for some valuable information about selecting one of these communities. Another helpful website is Consumer Consortium on Assisted Living (www.ccal.org).

MOVING TO ANOTHER GEOGRAPHIC AREA

While most people opt to stay in their same geographic area, you might be interested in relocating to another city or state for your primary or secondary residence. Perhaps the idea of moving to someplace where the cost of living might be lower appeals to you. Prices for food, utilities, health care and other necessities can also vary significantly in different areas of the country. Some states are more tax friendly than others. When weighing the merits of such a move, you need to consider all forms of taxes. This would include real estate, sales and even inheritance taxes. Some states don't tax retirement income. If you do choose to move to a lower tax state, be sure to keep good records to document your residency should the state you leave want to challenge your tax status.

Some retirees choose to move to be nearer family and friends— or to a warmer climate. Wherever you think you want to move, we recommend you consider renting there first for several months, while keeping your current residence, so you haven't cut off all your options. Leaving old friends and familiar places behind may not work for you.

Second Homes

Should you decide to age in place, you might want to rent or buy a second residence in another area. Many people who live in the north like to have a warmer place to go in the cold months. Eventually some move their primary residence to the warmer climate for tax or cost-of-living reasons. Here again, we recommend before you sell your current home, you rent a place for at least a year to see if you like living there in all seasons.

Conversely, prior to retirement you may have maintained two or more homes. Now that you are retired you may decide to simplify your life and reduce expenses by settling on one residence.

Recreational Vehicles

For those who want to travel around the country and have the comfort of a home, owning a recreational vehicle (RV) might be appealing. You might even decide to sell your existing home and use the RV as your primary residence. Some retirees use the RV as a second home. In this case they might park the RV in a retirement community in a warmer climate in the winter or they may move around the country visiting various RV parks. Typically, we find this approach is most appealing in the early stages of retirement.

If living in a RV appeals to you, we suggest renting before buying as this purchase can involve a major financial commitment.

RETIRING OUTSIDE THE UNITED STATES

For the more adventurous, retiring outside the United States is an option—not necessarily forever, but perhaps during the initial more active years of retirement. An organization that provides more information about this option is www.internationalliving.com.

TIMESHARES

Let's say you spend most of your time in one home. However, the idea of having another residence at least for a couple of weeks a year, might appeal to you. The answer might be buying a timeshare. If you decide to take this route, be very careful.

Timeshares involve an upfront cost of buying. Also, you must pay annual maintenance fees, which usually increase each year. Don't delude yourself that these are good investments, because if you try to sell your time share you may not be able to do so. If you are, it will sell for considerably less than what you paid for it. If you're interested in a given property, we recommend renting from an existing timeshare owner to see how much you like it. If you do decide to buy a timeshare, the best way is to buy directly from other timeshare owners who no longer want to pay their annual maintenance fees.

OTHER CONSIDERATIONS

SELL OR RENT?

You may decide that you no longer want to own a home but prefer to rent instead. This way you'd free up the money that is tied up in your home and invest it elsewhere or use it to support your lifestyle. There's a website that compares the economic choice of renting versus buying (www.trulia.com/rentvsbuy).

Costs Of Moving

If you decide to move, you need to factor in the costs of moving. Expenses to be considered are: the realtor fees, improvements and renovations needed to sell your current home, moving costs, enhancements to the new home and the tax implications of the sale.

A few helpful hints when dealing with a moving company. Rates are usually lower mid-week and mid-month. They also can be lower in September or later in the year. Make sure the movers visit your home to make an estimate. Ideally, get three estimates before making a decision (www.protectyourmove.gov).

As for the tax implications of the sale, under current law you owe no taxes if you have lived in your primary residence two out of the last five years and sell your house for a profit of $250,000 if you're single, or $500,000 as a married couple. If widowed, the surviving spouse may exclude up to $500,000 of the gain, if the residence is sold no later than two years after the spouse's death. When figuring your cost, you need to include home improvements.

How To Sell Your Home

While the idea of selling your home yourself and saving the real estate commission might be tempting, we would strongly recommend you use a realtor when you sell your home. As with the selection of any professional, pick a realtor who has had experience selling in your neighborhood and is prepared to represent you as the seller in the transaction.

Your realtor may recommend you use a home staging professional to prepare your house for sale. The object of this advice is to create a neutral environment so that the buyer can visualize herself in your home. It has been our experience that following this person's advice may speed the sale of your home at the price you want to achieve.

What To Do With All The Accumulated "Stuff"?

One of the major obstacles to moving is deciding what to do with all the stuff you have accumulated over the years. While the moving process may never be fun, there's no reason it has to be difficult. There are professionals who are trained to facilitate your move. They are called the National Association of Senior Move Managers (www.nasmm.org).

We find sorting through all your things that you have accumulated over the years can be the major obstacle preventing people from moving out of their homes. Intellectually you know it's the right thing to do, but emotionally you may find it difficult to let go. Readiness differs from one person to another.

Experts say the best way to face a large task such as this one is to tackle it in pieces. One approach is called the four-box system: 1) throw away, 2) appraise and sell unwanted items of value, 3) identify items you want to keep, and 4) donate items you no longer need or want. If you donate, we recommend you put together a written record of all the items, take pictures and provide realistic values for them in case the IRS chooses to audit your tax return. If you go to the Salvation Army website, they have a "Donation Value Guide" which will help you price your donations realistically.

If you still have more stuff than you can take with you, you can rent a storage unit for a year (you often get a price break that way). Then put all those things you don't have time to sort through now into the unit. This way you can go ahead with the move and take time afterward to sort through your possessions. Even if you decide not to move, aggressive decluttering can make life in your current home easier to manage.

TIMING YOUR MOVE

If you want to move to a retirement community versus aging in place—the question is when and where. The timing differs for everyone. Some choose to do it early in their retirement years. They're ready to leave their former lives behind and move to a new environment where they can make new friends and don't have to worry about household maintenance.

Others want to wait but plan to do so when they are older—say in their late seventies or early eighties. However, if you wait too long, health issues may prevent your admission. Alternatively, the place you want to go to may have too long a waiting list. It has been our experience that many people who finally make the move regret not doing so sooner. What's important is that you make the decision that you feel is right for you.

HOUSEHOLD INSURANCE

Whether you decide to stay in place or move, now is an excellent time to review your household and umbrella insurance to make sure it accurately reflects the value of your home and its contents as well as your net worth. Umbrella insurance is not expensive and is well worth it to provide you with peace of mind.

CONCLUSION

Keep in mind that your housing decisions may come in stages. If you have made a move when you first retire and then after a period of time, feel it's not the best for you, usually you're able to make a change. What works for you in the early stages of your retirement may not work later.

For instance, in your early years of retirement, you might continue to live in your current home. As time goes by, you may decide you prefer to live in an apartment since it is all on one floor and requires less maintenance than a single-family home. Later, you may decide you prefer the advantages of a retirement community.

Items To Consider Regarding Your Housing

- If you decide to stay in place, modify your home for future living.

- Consider sharing your home with someone else for income and/or companionship.

- If you choose to move, consider moving to an adult lifestyle community or a CCRC or some other place that requires less upkeep.

- If you move to another area, rent for a period of time before buying.

- Consider whether buying a second home or a recreational vehicle is desirable.

- Living outside the United States might be an attractive alternative.

- Seek professional advice before buying a timeshare.

- Review the option of renting versus owning.

- Budget for moving costs and settlement costs when selling.

- Keep in mind you will need time to sort through your "stuff" before moving.

- Update household insurance regularly.

CATHERINE CHAPTER SEVEN:
HOUSING

Catherine reflected on the last few months of her life. She couldn't believe how she and Jordan had gone from an employed couple who had done no retirement planning to one where they had become very financially engaged. They had known that eventually they would retire but hadn't make any plans. For two well-educated people, how could they have been so naïve?

Although Jordan losing his job had been a shock to both of them, in a way it also had been positive. They were forced to take a hard look at their situation and make plans for the future. In the past, her income was certainly nice to have, but now it was a necessity. They needed to have her income to make sure that they had a secure retirement. This was certainly a role reversal, since in the past Jordan's salary had been their primary income source.

One of the topics that she and Jordan had discussed with Joe was their housing. Obviously, the mortgage, taxes and maintenance of their home was a major expense. They had considered selling the beach house, but they really loved going down there and spending time with James and Amanda. They had a group of friends who went down there as well which provided them with an active social life.

Joe had discussed with them their desire to travel. They both had been so busy with their jobs they kept postponing taking any lengthy trips. Joe suggested they consider renting their beach house for a couple of weeks in August when they could get the maximum rent. According to the current tax law, the income wouldn't be taxable if they only rented it for 14 days, and then they could use the income to pay for their trip. That idea appealed to both of them since that way there wouldn't be any out-of-pocket cost. At the top of their "bucket list" was a trip to London and possibly Ireland and and to Scotland, where Catherine's ancestors originally came from. She really could get into planning a trip like this for the summer and it would give them something that both of them could look forward to doing.

Catherine was pleased that since Jordan was no longer working he'd been able to spend some time with his father. Both of them had concerns about Ben living alone at his age in New Jersey. The last time Jordan had visited his father he was able to persuade him to come down and stay with them during the coming winter months. Although New Jersey wasn't that far away, the winters were colder there than in the Washington, DC area. There were periods of time Ben couldn't leave his apartment because he feared falling on the ice. They had a comfortable guest room on the first floor with a full bathroom that would be perfect for him. They had already put grab bars in the shower so they wouldn't worry about him falling. Also, this way Jordan would have some company while he was sorting out what he was going to do with his future. Perhaps they could take on a father/son project or two. Ben had always been handy around the house.

As she was thinking of Jordan's dad's situation, it was natural that she would start thinking about her own parents. Prompted by Joe, she'd had a conversation with them with regard to their financial situation, and they assured her that they had sufficient resources to live comfortably. They didn't have a mortgage on their apartment so in the future if they decided they wanted to move to a retirement community they would have enough money to do so. However, for the time being they had made it clear that they wanted to age in place in their apartment. They had round-the-clock service at the front desk and it was in a safe neighborhood where they could walk most places they wanted to go. For further distances they could easily hail a cab or call for a driver. Catherine was greatly relieved that she didn't have to worry about them financially for the time being.

EMILY CHAPTER SEVEN:
HOUSING

A lot had happened to Emily in the last month. She, Hank and Carter had spent every weekend getting ready to sell the house. They'd made piles of items they might be able to sell, those they would give away and those they would throw away. Emily had considered an "estate" sale for the items she thought could be sold, but then a friend had told her about someone who could take care of this for her for a fee. This person said she would sell what she could, donate the rest to a charity and get a receipt for donated goods. That approach seemed a lot simpler to Emily and certainly much less time consuming.

While Emily was in the process of dealing with her house sale, she and Hank started looking at apartments. Hank had put together a list of what each of them wanted in an apartment and they had gone over it together. She had told him that it was important to her to have a modern spacious kitchen and a master bedroom with a bathroom with two sinks. She thought they needed at least one bedroom in addition to the master bedroom, which they could make into an office/den for Hank. Ideally, they would have three bedrooms so their children or grandchildren could stay overnight if they wanted to do so on occasion. On the other hand, she realized that they could put a sleep sofa in the den, which would take care of that need. She also wanted a front desk person on duty 24 hours per day. She told Hank this would make her feel safer when he traveled as he had to do periodically. He agreed with all this but also wanted to make sure the apartment would be close to restaurants and other services such as cleaners and drugstores. They both wanted underground parking for their two cars.

After living in the suburbs all these years, Emily was ready to experience living somewhere where you could walk rather than drive to get someplace. She was happy that Hank shared her feelings in this regard.

She knew that moving from a large house to an apartment would be a big adjustment for her. However, when she compared the square footage of the house with the apartments they had seen, it wasn't that much different—it was just more efficiently laid out. Certainly, the idea of living in an apartment where everything was on one floor was very appealing.

Last weekend they had found an apartment that they thought would work for them. It had a large living/dining area and a modern kitchen. The master bedroom was roomy with a walk-in closet. The bathroom had two sinks and the second bedroom had a full bath as well. Hank could use that as his den. He already called it his "man cave"! Emily was ready to get rid of much of her current furniture. After all, most of it had been bought when she married Doug. She looked forward to having modern and sleeker pieces of furniture that would be more suitable for an apartment. What she particularly liked about the apartment was the large windows. Since it was on the corner of the building there was lots of light. There was a small balcony that was big enough for a table and a couple of chairs where they could have coffee in the morning.

Hank and Emily also had discussed an appropriate financial arrangement. He told her as a partner in the accounting firm that he was in good financial shape despite the cost of his divorce and his alimony payments. His income was about twice what hers would be after she left her current job and her alimony ended. On the other hand, once the house was sold, she would have that money to invest and provide her with additional income. Hank suggested he pay two thirds the cost of their apartment and she could pay one third. Emily thought his suggestion was more than generous. She truly appreciated it and agreed to this initial arrangement. How different this agreement was from when Doug paid for everything. She liked the feeling of being a partner with Hank.

After all these years in her current home, the concept of low maintenance was very appealing to Emily. Renting the apartment would make economic sense while Hank was still paying alimony. It would give them a chance to get used to living together and also time to look around and see what kind of housing and neighborhood they might want to select in the future.

Hank's apartment lease would be up in three months. She thought the house would be ready to be put on the market about the same time. In the meantime they decided to sign the lease on the new apartment and start looking for some basic furniture, such as a bed for their bedroom, a sofa bed and desk for the den. She was really tired of her furniture. The furniture Hank had was pretty basic and not really worth keeping. As for other things such as kitchen equipment, silver, glasses and plates, she had more than enough for them. Emily had gone from dreading the move and all it entailed to really looking forward to her new life with Hank. It truly was going to be a great adventure!

MELISSA CHAPTER SEVEN:
HOUSING

After Melissa had explained to David why she really wasn't ready to make a full time move to Florida, he'd been much more understanding. He admitted the reason he wanted to live in Florida was motivated by his desire to escape the cold Michigan weather. He now realized he hadn't given much thought to living there in the summer, which would be hotter than Michigan. He also recognized that he'd been so busy with his job that he hadn't understood how much time she'd been spending meeting the needs of her parents and Hannah. Although Melissa wasn't averse to spending some time in Florida this winter, she confessed to David that she didn't want to live right next door to her in-laws. She liked her father-in-law, but her mother-in-law could be a little difficult at times. She always seemed to have a better way to do things than Melissa. At this point in her life, Melissa didn't think she could put up with that for too long.

She and David had a frank discussion about these issues. They reviewed the information the realtor had given them about the sale of their current home. They had looked at the townhouse models that Melissa had seen in the paper, and it appeared they could find something that would suit their needs for less than what they expected to receive from the sale of their house.

After talking further about the feasibility of having two homes, they decided to start with the sale of their current home and the purchase of a smaller one in Michigan. At the same time, David would take a trip down to visit his parents in Sarasota and find out what three-month winter rental options were available to them. Melissa was reassured when David pointed out that some of their friends had already settled in the Sarasota area, so their social life didn't have to revolve around his parents. There was a golf club they could join, and he could play golf with his cronies all day every day if he chose to do so. Melissa suspected that he might find that it might get old after awhile, but if that is what he wanted to do, that is what he should do. The plan would be that he would be there from January to March and she would be there part of that time.

Melissa thought this was a good plan of action. She realized that in order to sell the house she would need to weed through all the "stuff" they had accumulated over the years. She'd already started to do this, but there was much more to do. She recognized that although David could sort out his home office most of the other work was up to her.

Now that they had a plan, Melissa thought it would be a good time to update their son Chris and his wife Jean. Since she and Hannah spent more time together, Hannah was aware of their potential move, but since she didn't see as much of Chris and Jean they weren't as up to speed with their plans. Considering the changes on the horizon in connection with David's retirement, she wanted to discuss with them whether she and David could spend more time with Hannah's children on the weekends when she was in Florida.

As for her parents, she wanted to update them as well. She had had a conversation with them about their considering a move to a retirement community and was pleased to learn they were positive about the idea. They told her that recently they had had lunch and toured a nearby facility where some of their friends lived. They'd already downsized once by moving to their current home ten years ago, so this wouldn't be that much of a transition for them. Her mother admitted she was tired of cooking all the meals and taking care of the house and yard. Although she had help, it would be nice to have all that taken care of for them. Also, their friends said that they really liked the social life. There was a lot to do at the retirement community and transportation to activities at other locations was provided. If they had doctor or other appointments, there was a service that would drive them there and back. Since it was a continuing care facility, if they had some serious health issues, assistance would be provided.

Melissa was greatly relieved by this conversation. It appeared that her parents were well on their way to making a move on their own. She had been worried about how they would get to their various appointments if she was in Florida or what would happen if one of them fell in their home and went to the hospital. If they moved to the retirement community, she would know they were safe and able to receive the necessary care. She'd been willing to drive them and her grandchildren around when David was working and she had the free time to do it. Now that he was retiring, she wanted to spend more time with him. Living in a warmer climate in the winter appealed to her. Also, she would like to travel more. In the past, they had to limited their travel to David's work schedule. They even might drive down to Florida, stopping to see friends and sights on the way.

Victoria Chapter Seven:
Housing

A week after participating in her final graduation ceremony and saying the goodbyes to her students and fellow faculty members, Victoria sat down with John and reviewed her retirement plan. As he promised, he'd developed two options for her. What she anticipated was correct. She really couldn't afford to move to San Francisco unless she was willing to downsize to a much smaller place. In addition, the real estate taxes would be higher than she was currently paying. Although she really didn't need all the space she currently had, she liked having it. The idea of city life still appealed to her, but she knew she would miss sitting and reading in her backyard, small as it was. If she moved to the city, she would have less money for travel. This would be a problem, since she'd been looking forward to expanding her travel options when she had more free time.

John pointed out that she had the basement in her townhouse, which could be modified to be rented to a student or to another professor. That would be another source of income to her as well as provide some companionship. He explained she could use some of her inheritance money to finance the renovation. At the same time, she could modernize her own kitchen and the bathrooms. This idea of having someone in the house when she took extended trips appealed to her.

As for giving up her pipe dream of living in the city, Victoria looked at her lists and realized that although the city offered a lot in the way of culture, so did Berkeley. She had looked at the adult education courses offered by the university and found several that appealed to her. She had started to spend more time with members of the writers group and realized she had a lot in common with several of them, more than she had when she was still working. She had gone to plays with one member and concerts with another. She hadn't had time for many of these activities when she was still working. It wasn't as if where she was living was a cultural wasteland! Rather than living in the city, it was an easy commute to San Francisco, and she could stay in a bed and breakfast for a week or so if she wanted to binge on theatre and/or museums. That would cost a lot less than moving to the city. Since she lived nearby, she could have her cake and eat it too!

So, the decision really boiled down to choices. With John's help, she'd decided that being able to take extensive trips when she wanted to was more important to her than moving to the city, where money would be tight. Actually, that was an easy decision. She lived in a comfortable home which she could make even more comfortable. She had plenty of stimulating opportunities available to her in her current environment and if the spirit moved her, she could stay in the city for a week or so.

Next step—find a contractor and determine what it would cost to make some improvements to her home. When she modernized her bathrooms, she thought she would add some grab bars and possibly a bench in her shower. She didn't need them now but eventually she probably would, and if she was going to "age in place," it felt good to plan ahead. Although she wasn't looking forward to the disruption that the renovation would entail, she thought the end result would be worth it.

Chapter Eight

Emotional And Social Adjustment

Ready or not, you now find yourself out of the workforce or your former routine and into the first phase of your active retirement. Planned or unexpected, you are there. As you wake up this first morning, undoubtedly there will be many thoughts going through your mind. You might be thinking, "Hooray, I'm going to do absolutely nothing today. I'm going to get up whenever I want and drink a cup of coffee while I watch a morning TV show. Next, I am going to take a long shower, get dressed and decide what I'm going to do with the rest of my day." You might choose to work out at the gym, go shopping for yourself, spend time watching a movie or reading a book. Whatever you choose to do, you now have the luxury of not having to do something at a particular time or follow a schedule other than one of your own making.

On the other hand, on that first day, some of you are going to jump right in and begin reviewing the lists you have made of things that you've waited to do until you actually retired. This may include making phone calls about volunteer activities you had in mind or prioritizing which projects in your home you want to tackle first as well as other "when I'm retired" items. Regardless of how you're feeling about your new status, now is the time to get started involving yourself in some of the things you've been anticipating doing when you retired.

EMOTIONAL CONSIDERATIONS

How a new retiree reacts to the first day of retirement varies widely. Suffice it to say that they run the gamut of emotions experienced when one is at the point of any major life transition. Whatever you're feeling, realize that you're not alone. Keep in mind that currently, ten thousand people retire each day. Others are having similar feelings to you as they enter this new chapter of their lives. Charting your course so that it includes activities to look forward to as well as ones to stimulate your mind will result in a more satisfied retirement life. Finding a way to create a balance among the various aspects of your life is key.

Whether retirement was something you opted for or was unexpected, you can make the most of it. For instance, start by identifying one activity that you truly enjoy that's available in your area and spend some time doing it without feeling guilty. For example, if you've always valued reading and felt you never had enough time to enjoy that activity, give some thought to what you would like to do with that interest. Would you like to join a book club? Do you want to take a literature class at a community college or online? Perhaps reading to children, the elderly or to people with vision issues would appeal to you—to name but a few options.

If you're married or in a long-time partnership, you may find that you and your partner or significant other are on the same page with regard to your hopes and dreams for your retirement years. If so, that's great and you should be on your way to a mutually rewarding time together.

If, however, you have one idea and your partner an entirely different one, you may be wondering how you are going to survive spending so much time together. If your partner has been working and you have not, you may feel that your turf is being invaded and your routine disrupted. Your partner may be excited to try an activity with you, while you may be dreading it. Recognize that you don't have to be joined at the hip. Instead, it might be beneficial for each of you to pursue some of your individual interests. For instance, your partner may hate the opera and you love it. A solution would be for you to go to the opera with friends, while your partner does something else. Pursuing individual activities usually brings increased vitality to your relationship.

Unfortunately, in some instances, couples who've been together for years sometimes discover that when they're retired and together all the time, they actually have little in common. You may find that the idea of spending the rest of your lives together, which could be as long as thirty more years, isn't appealing. It's somewhat surprising, but also sad that there's a high incidence of divorce among new retirees as they face the reality of their future together. Over the years you've grown apart. Perhaps without realizing it you've been living separate lives for years. There is no simple answer about what to do in this type of situation. Every couple needs to make a determination as what is best to do moving forward.

It's never advisable to make a rash decision with regard to maintaining or dissolving a long-term relationship. Change is destabilizing and impacts every aspect of your life. Take time to explore the viability of your existing relationship. The demands of daily life prior to retirement may have resulted in your going through the motions of life focused on just talking about routine matters such as appointments, family issues, social obligations and work demands. You may have become detached and removed from what brought you together in the first place.

There are counselors practicing in most urban areas who can help you assess your relationship, looking at your compatibility and suggesting ways to improve your communication with one another. This relationship counselor will work with you to assess the pros and cons of your specific relationship and identify ways to reconnect. Alternatively, she may reinforce the idea that your situation has deteriorated to such an extent that it will prevent you from feeling fulfilled in your life together. Should that be the case, she will also guide you through the process to disengage in a collaborative way with hopefully minimal anger or antagonism. The most difficult situation to address is when one party wants to maintain the status quo and the other does not. Regardless of the outcome, you owe it to yourself to seek professional help. Keep in mind that as with your financial decisions, consulting those with expertise in the area under consideration is invaluable.

SOCIALIZATION

This is also a good time to assess how much activity and socialization is right for you.

If you were working, you may have found it necessary to belong to several organizations related to your work. Some may be the result of associations you've formed with the parents of some of your children's friends, some may be the result of ongoing interests that you've maintained throughout the years, still others may be due to joint activities such as tennis or bridge. Your concern here is twofold. One is: Will I still fit in? The other is: Do I really want to continue doing this activity? A common concern is the former.

By this time, you should have sorted out which prior friendships you'll continue to maintain. As you find yourself actively retired, you have time to explore new activities and meet new people with whom you may find you will have much in common. This may result in your making new friends. For example, in the past you might not have had time to take a yoga class, because they always seemed to be held in the mornings when you were unavailable or in the evening when you were too tired. You might try to take one now. You may find yourself participating in the class with women of varied ages. Perhaps you'll meet someone who is at a similar point in life with whom you share interests. If so, pursue the contact. Suggest having a cup of coffee or tea after class and go from there. If it works out great, if not, nothing lost.

Now that your daily schedule is not determined by others, you can focus on yourself and what feels comfortable and right for you. With your newfound freedom, you don't have to maintain activities that you no longer enjoy. Be true to yourself!

As you assess this new chapter of your life, review the varied activities you've enjoyed in the past. If you've valued being active in an organization, stay involved. If you'd always dreaded attending meetings and related command performances, give yourself permission to step down and investigate something new. There're no absolutes here.

Start by giving some thought to things you enjoy without feeling guilty. Identify what allows you to function best. Are you someone who loves spontaneity and has always felt smothered by the tasks you were responsible for on a daily basis? Well, now is the time to allow yourself to do something on the spur of the moment. Perhaps you just want to take a day to go to a museum, or go on a drive with no specific destination in mind or a movie in the morning. This is the time you can indulge yourself.

On the other hand, you might be someone who needs structure in order to feel comfortable. Perhaps losing the structure imposed by the outside world might be unsettling. You might have felt more secure when life was more predictable. If this is so, give some thought to creating your own structure. Try to create a new pattern, blending new and familiar practices. It's time to develop a plan that will allow you to integrate new activities into your life. At the same time, don't abandon the patterns of your life that have allowed you to feel comfortable and secure. This is not an all or nothing process. Rather you should explore that which works best for you in your newfound space. When trying to assess the choices ahead, you may find technology to be a helpful resource.

There are many doors you can open. Try not to allow yourself to commit to just one activity, preventing you from exploring other options which might be available and of considerable interest to you. Since you were tied to schedules, deadlines and meeting the needs of others in the past, this may feel like an alien concept. Now we're suggesting that you need to move away from that type of thought process and focus on yourself.

Perhaps, as you navigate these unfamiliar waters, you might have a difficult time determining the right combination of new experiences and new people to take on without giving up some of the things you've enjoyed in the past. Certainly, if you've always enjoyed participating in a given activity, we're not suggesting you end your involvement, but instead we're suggesting that you maintain that activity but add something that is new and hopefully mentally stimulating.

FAMILY RELATIONSHIPS

If you have grandchildren, and you live near them, it's likely that you've been actively involved in their lives. At this phase of your retirement, you may want to expand your role with them. This may be a great opportunity for both you and your grandchildren. Spending time with them shouldn't be limited to driving them to their activities, but also doing something mutually rewarding and interactive.

Frequently when reading about how a successful individual's interest in a given area was sparked, it's attributed to the role played by a grandparent. Lessons for life are sometimes provided by grandparents in a way not available to parents. Both grandparents and grandchildren benefit from spending time together. However, on the other hand, we'd encourage you not to let your children and grandchildren monopolize your life.

When extended family members realize that you are more available to do things with and for them, they may expect you to provide them with more of your time. You may already be helping out in many ways, but now that you have additional free time, you may feel compelled to do more.

The beginning of your active retirement is a good time for you to determine how much time you're comfortable giving to your family members. Once you have made this decision, make sure your family is aware. Boundaries and limits are critical. It will be beneficial for all if you do so. Doing things because you feel guilty about not doing them isn't healthy for you or anyone else. This type of dilemma may increase the likelihood of experiencing anxiety or depression.

Socializing with family and friends, expanding old interests, developing new interests, remaining physically and mentally active are all components of an enriched life in retirement.

PETS

You may be one of those people who has always longed to have a pet but felt that the demands of work and family precluded providing a pet with sufficient time and attention, so you opted not to have one. Now with the change in your routine you do have the time to devote to a pet and are looking forward to what the pet may add to your life.

One caution here. Don't go overboard at the outset. Select a pet that you feel you can manage and see how it goes. Don't get talked into taking two dogs or cats from the same litter if it is suggested. Be very clear on what is involved in caring for your pet and how this will impact your life. Also, be aware of the costs involved. You'll have not only the cost of the food, but regular visits to the vet and other expenses. On the other hand, being involved with a pet can provide companionship and the opportunity to meet other animal lovers. Pets can be a positive addition to your life—they're always happy to see you!

As a reminder, you don't want to find yourself tied to the demands of your pet so that it interferes with your doing some of the things you have been looking forward to doing, such as travel. Now that you have time to enjoy and investigate new areas of interest you might not want to be tied to yet another obligation. You want a pet to add fulfillment to your life, not control it. If you find yourself moving in the direction of allowing your pet to determine what you do, take some time to think about why you are doing this to yourself.

Spirituality And Religion

Usually there're a variety of activities provided to the members of most organized religions in addition to the existing weekly services. There are youth groups, discussion groups, bible study groups, services provided to the elderly, and instructional classes for children to name but a few. Your newfound unscheduled time might allow you to participate in this type of activity and probably let you meet other members of the congregation whom you may not have known previously, resulting in new friendships. It also provides an opportunity to be of service to those less fortunate, which may be personally rewarding.

You might want to take a class on religion, spirituality or philosophy offered by a university in your geographic area or attend programs sponsored by the members of a particular religious denomination. This may be something you and your partner have always wanted to do together or it may be something you're interested in doing on your own. If so, feel comfortable meeting your own need.

As you move toward the final chapter of your life, spirituality and religion may become increasingly more important to you. If so, it's incumbent on you to explore this area to your own satisfaction. However the journey turns out, it'll be well worth the time you have put into it. In all likelihood you'll feel better about where you find yourself at this juncture in your life.

Items To Consider As You Make Emotional And Social Adjustments

- You may choose to relax and enjoy the freedom of no schedule or you may want structure.

- Since you are spending more time with your partner, there will be adjustments.

- If you're having trouble adapting to this new chapter in your life, seek professional help.

- Continue to explore opportunities to establish new friendships that will enrich your life while maintaining and renewing former meaningful relationships.

- Don't take on more responsibility with your family than you can handle emotionally and financially.

- You may want to buy a pet now that you have more time to spend with it.

- If you're so inclined, explore religion and spirituality further.

Catherine Chapter Eight:
Emotional And Social Adjustments

Catherine was waiting for Amanda to arrive for their planned day of shopping. She had just completed her first semester of law school. Jordan and Catherine had been able to give her some financial help with the tuition and she had been able to secure loans for what her parents couldn't cover. It had worked out well. Amanda seemed to really be enjoying her classes and on occasion engaged her parents in discussions about a point of law she was learning. Since she was attending law school in the Washington, DC, area, they'd actually begun to see more of Amanda which they all enjoyed.

Jordan had followed the employment counselor, Judy Byrne's advice and investigated some nonprofits whose work appealed to him. The Boys and Girls Club did just that because of its mission, which was "to enable all young people, especially those who need us most, to reach their full potential as productive, caring, responsible citizens." He visited the local club and was impressed with the work they were doing to motivate and educate young people.

He began to volunteer at the club two days a week working both with the kids and the management in order to better understand the work of the organization. It opened his eyes to an entirely different world. After a month of volunteering, Jessica Johnson, one of the board members, asked him to help her to review their bylaws because she knew he was an attorney. He was pleased that she had approached him with the project. It really was an ego boost for him.

He wondered how she had time to volunteer for the Boys and Girls Club because he knew she was a successful realtor working on her own. In the course of their work on the project she told him that she'd actually been a latch key kid when she was growing up. In 1990 the Boys Club had expanded to become the Boys and Girls Club. When she was in high school, she had been a beneficiary of their programs and credited the organization for truly saving her life and pointing her in the right direction. So, although she was busy in her career, she wanted to give back in some way for the help she'd received in her youth.

When they had finished the first draft of the bylaws revision, Jessica asked him to lunch. She explained that her real estate practice had grown to the point that it was almost more than she could handle by herself. She specialized in selling older homes in his Chevy Chase neighborhood, a suburb of Washington, DC. She had several younger people working for her who handled a lot of the follow-up detail work. She was the "rainmaker" and the "closer" but she thought she could use some help from someone more mature. The fact that he was a lawyer appealed to her. She asked if he might have any interest in joining her. She thought their personalities complimented each other and they seemed to work well together. If so, she would encourage him to take the real estate licensing class.

Jordan had never considered working in real estate but now thought it sounded like it might be a good option for him. He was interested in the way Jessica described her business and thought it was something that he might enjoy doing. He could take the course while he was still receiving his severance pay, and see how it went. To his surprise he enjoyed it. He passed the real estate exam and now he and Jessica were working together.

Catherine was relieved that Jordan now had a source of income and was feeling good about what he was doing. Getting into real estate made him more aware of a number of improvement and repairs that needed to be done at their home. When both of them were working they hadn't had time to focus on the house. After Ben had moved in, Jordan and his dad began to work on some of these projects together. Father and son appreciated each other and valued the time they spent together. The three months they'd anticipated his staying with them stretched into more months. Eventually they all agreed that he should move in with them on a full-time basis. They hadn't worked out all the details with regard to the move, but the decision had been made. Catherine's parents made an effort to spend some time with Ben. As a result, they introduced him to some other people so he developed a social life of his own.

There had been so many changes in their lives that although Catherine and Jordan had agreed to take that two-week trip to England, Scotland and Ireland they hadn't done so yet. They'd made plans to do so but had agreed to postpone it to the following spring. This gave them more time to work on their plans and had brought them closer together. They did rent out the beach house for two weeks in August as Joe had recommended. During the rest of the summer they were able to enjoy the beach with family and friends.

Ben had also helped Jordan with some minor repairs to the beach house. One of the unexpected pluses of all of this was that Ben had a chance to get to know Amanda and James as people in their own right. Both grandchildren and Ben clearly benefitted. What had left Jordan initially emotionally paralyzed had turned out to be a plus for the entire family. None of them would ever have predicted that to be the case.

EMILY CHAPTER EIGHT:
EMOTIONAL AND SOCIAL AJDUSTMENTS

Emily couldn't believe how much her life had changed this past year. First and foremost, she was no longer working at the nonprofit she had worked at for years. The board had given her a retirement party, and it made her feel good to know that she had been appreciated. At first it had felt strange not to be working a five-day week, but she was adjusting. Actually, she was enjoying her newfound freedom and not being tied down to a 9 to 5 schedule.

It had been a busy year. As previously noted, she and Hank had found a great apartment. She'd sold her house for the asking price and waded through the accumulated stuff of her life with Doug and beyond. Jill had come to Georgia for one long weekend to help her mother with the sorting, which was very meaningful to both of them. Although Jill didn't want much of the furniture that her mother had, she did take some of the things that were important to her from her life before marriage.

To Emily's surprise, Carter had asked her if he could have some of the furniture put in a storage unit. He said that he didn't need anything else now, but that he thought that at some point in the future he might be ready to have his own apartment. At that time, it would be helpful for him to have some of this furniture to use to get him started. He told her that he was earning enough money to pay for a small storage unit so it wouldn't cost her anything. Basically, Emily was thrilled to know that Carter was thinking ahead in this way.

From her perspective, it represented real growth. Within the past month, he'd actually introduced her to Louise, a young woman he'd begun to date. UNBELIEVABLE PROGRESS!

Emily and Hank had furnished their new apartment with a combination of his and her things as well as new things. She was very pleased with the end result. She felt their apartment was welcoming and required a fraction of the upkeep of her former home.

After they moved, she joined a health club near where they lived and finally took a yoga class. There was quite an age range in the class so she didn't feel too conspicuous. She identified another woman who she thought might be a retiree. After the third class, Emily approached her and suggested they have a smoothie together. She agreed. They went to the center's coffee shop and ended up talking for hours. She discovered that Carla indeed had recently retired. She'd been a special education teacher for years and was also enjoying her newfound ability to do something in the morning. She and her husband had four adult children who were scattered around the country. One thing led to another, and before Emily realized it, they had begun to spend the time after the yoga class together on a regular basis.

Emily also found that she had more time to spend with her longstanding friends from the ADHD support group. These women had gone through so much together when the children were growing up. It was good to find out how they all were doing now.

Since she had left her full-time job, she'd been fortunate to be able to do some consulting work with a couple of other nonprofit organizations. However, she wanted to do fundraising work for one organization, which she could do part-time, but on a regular basis. It was important to her that the work be personally rewarding and at the same time provide her with some predictable income. Understanding as ever, Hank had told her to take as much time as she needed to find the right job.

Both Hank and Emily were very happy about the way they had been able to blend their families. The adult children on both sides had been so accepting of Hank and Emily's decision to move forward with their relationship. All the adult children had come to the apartment for their housewarming party. Jill and Harvey's children really seemed to get along with each other, which was remarkable given the age differences. Jill also got to spend some time with Carter and Louise. All the adult children involved assured them that they would try to make time to spend together during the holidays. Even Jill, who adored her father, Doug, was very complimentary of Hank and how good he seemed to be for her mother.

Carter had volunteered to work with Olivia's soccer team since he'd played the sport for years when he was younger. Hank's grandchildren even asked if they could spend an overnight with Emily and Hank sometime since they lived so close to where they liked to shop.

All in all, it was a much better beginning than she had anticipated. Hank's relaxed manner made such a difference. It was really amazing. First and foremost, she thought what made her relationship with Hank so positive was her current sense of self. She had come so far from that wide-eyed girl who was swept off her feet by Doug. She and Doug had been happy in the beginning because she rarely disagreed with any of Doug's opinions and requests. However, in contrast to her relationship with Doug, she recognized that her relationship with Hank was actually a mature one where they were able to have conversations as equals valuing each other's opinions. She felt so fortunate.

MELISSA CHAPTER EIGHT:
EMOTIONAL AND SOCIAL ADJUSTMENTS

What a year this had been! David had gone down to Florida and located an apartment that was reasonably close to his parents but not next door. They'd agreed that they would need a three-bedroom unit so that they could have both Hannah and Chris's families visit them.

David hadn't made a snap decision. He'd looked at many units and selected the one which he thought best met their needs. They'd agreed that initially they would rent. This particular unit was a rental with an option to buy. Melissa told David that she would like to see it first before he signed the lease. She volunteered to fly down for a weekend. When she boarded the plane she realized that she had never flown by herself before. David had really been protective of her. Definitely time to be a grown up!

They also had agreed to purchase a townhouse in Bloomfield Hills, which was near where Hannah lived. Hannah and her kids and Chris and his kids came to help sort through all the stuff that they had accumulated during their growing up years. They had lots of laughs as they looked at some of the things they couldn't part with from their childhood. David and Melissa had decided to rent a storage unit to hold some of their furniture they didn't need now but might come in handy for one of the grandchildren in a first apartment. It was a lot of work but also rewarding.

Her parents had moved into the retirement community in the Detroit area where some of their friends lived. During the first winter Melissa went back and forth to Detroit from Sarasota with regularity. As time went on, she found herself wanting to stay longer in Florida instead of dealing with the cold.

Her personal social life hadn't changed much. Several of their friends had relocated to the Sarasota area so she had a ready-made group of people with whom to socialize. One of her friends introduced her to a church similar to the one they'd belonged to in Detroit. She and David took an immediate liking to the pastor and the other members of the congregation. Since she volunteered to work in the church she made some new friends. Church had always been important to her and she didn't want to lose that connection in her new life. Going to church always helped her feel centered.

David seemed to enjoy going to church with her and it had become a special part of their life together. Wherever they were, they went to church services on Sunday and then out to brunch. It was a meaningful time for them. Despite her concern about the changes in her life this first year, she'd done better than she'd anticipated doing. They'd settled into their two new homes. David seemed to be thriving in the warmer weather. He really was enjoying being able to play golf several times a week. They had joined a small golf club where some of their friends belonged. They did see her in-laws occasionally but it wasn't a constant. David also made a point of going to see them on his own.

Her most difficult adjustment was not being able to see Hannah's children several times a week. She really missed them. She did make a point of FaceTiming with them regularly, but it wasn't quite the same as spending time driving them to and from activities and sharing impromptu dinners.

Chris and his family had made an effort to spend at least one weekend a month with Hannah and her children. They tried to plan activities that might be of interest to the varied ages involved. Both of her children made a point of visiting their grandparents in the retirement community, which she really appreciated.

Hannah had made some adjustments of her own since Melissa was no longer available to help out. Given Hannah's salary she was able to hire a young college student to do the afternoon driving of her children and even start their dinner. Both Tad and Alexa seemed to really like her and she was very responsible. She frequently shared anecdotes with them about her own growing up years, which they seemed to find amusing. For example, she'd never seen snow before she moved to Michigan!

Even their dog, Taffy, had adjusted to their two-home situation. They really hadn't considered what they were going to do with Taffy when they were thinking about their housing changes. Close to the time when they'd agreed that they would drive one of their cars down to Florida they looked at each other and said at the same time, "But what about Taffy?" Taffy was nine years old. Neither of their children was in a position to take her. They finally decided to just take her with them and see how she did. In Florida, Taffy initially wasn't too sure about apartment living, but soon grew acclimated to her new surroundings and loved to stretch out on their balcony in the sun. Taffy also adjusted well to having two homes.

Victoria Chapter Eight:
Emotional And Social Adjustments

Victoria looked around her newly remodeled basement. It certainly was nothing like what it previously had been. After interviewing several contractors she'd hired one who'd been highly recommended and also seemed to understand her vision for the space. Together they'd worked out that the basement would have a large all-purpose living area plus a bedroom, bath and kitchen with a fairly small outside patio. His estimate was more than she'd initially wanted to spend but wasn't that bad. As she soon learned, the time frame suggested did not materialize because of a variety of delays. For instance, the material sent was not what was ordered, or the manufacturer needed more time to meet the request, because they'd run out of stock. She accepted the fact that these delays were to be expected. Most of the people she knew who'd undertaken something like this had experienced similar glitches. Therefore, she didn't take it personally or think the contractor had taken advantage of her because she was a woman.

The end result exceeded her expectations. She didn't regret for one minute her decision to stay where she was in Berkeley. She found that she enjoyed her home even more now that she had more time to spend there. She hadn't rented out the space yet as had been her original intent. It was still her plan to do so, but for the moment, she couldn't decide whether she would prefer to rent to a college student or an older woman. While it might be nice to have a younger person around who could help with some of the household chores, she might relate better to someone closer to her own age. Victoria felt certain she would begin the process of looking for someone to rent to before the next semester began.

She did go to San Francisco on a regular basis. Sometimes she stayed with her sister and other times she stayed at a charming Bed and Breakfast located not too far from Winnie. They went to plays and museums and walked around the city. Sometimes they just enjoyed wandering and poking around unfamiliar places. Of course, they went to new and familiar restaurants as well as allowing themselves to spend some time shopping.

These visits were in addition to the holidays, which she'd routinely shared with Winnie and her family. During the past year she'd convinced her mother to accompany her, which she thought had been very beneficial for all. Winnie's boys did not get too many opportunities to spend time with their grand-mother and this gave them a chance to get to know her better.

Victoria continued to spend more time with members of the writers group. One of her friends in this group got her involved with the local community theater group. She'd agreed to take on a very small role in their spring production. She only had a few lines but found that she liked being a partici-pant rather than just being a spectator. She'd made some new friends there and had agreed to become more involved this coming fall. She wasn't sure in what capacity, but she liked the environment.

In the midst of the work on the house, she'd been contacted by the travel coordinator at her university to see if she would be willing to take on the leadership of the student trip they had planned for Mexico during spring break. One of the other professors who had been planning on leading the trip had to cancel due to a family medical issue. The travel coordinator realized that it was very short notice and didn't know if Victoria would be able to take it on, but she did know that she had the necessary expertise. She also told her if she could manage the time frame, they would pay all her expenses.

Victoria actually was thrilled with this offer. She and Rodney had discussed going to Tulum in Mexico to explore some of the Mayan sites in greater detail this coming year but hadn't made any definite plans yet. This trip would give her an opportunity to spend some time in Mexico and get a better idea as to what might work for them. She didn't hesitate for very long before agreeing to take on the ten-day trip. Victoria was really excited.

CHAPTER NINE

Physical And Mental Health Adjustment

Medical Factors

*B*y now we assume you've sorted out your health insurance coverage. If you're age 65 or older, it's likely you have in place your Medicare and any other supplemental coverage you may need to provide you with optimum health protection.

It's important to review your existing coverage on an annual basis. As a reminder, open season for Medicare D prescription coverage takes place annually from mid-October to early December. This provides you with an opportunity to review your existing prescription drug coverage. Now that you're fully retired, you should be in a better position to assess your coverage and modify it to meet your personal needs if necessary. If you want further information you can call and speak to someone at either Medicare or AARP to go over the pros and cons of what you currently have as well as the implications of making any changes to your initial coverage. The key here is: a) to understand what you have in place and b) to determine if it meets your needs.

Choices Of Medical Practitioners

Now is also a good time to consider whether your medical providers are appropriate for your current situation. As you age, it may be advisable to change to doctors who are younger than you and are willing to assume the responsibility for your medical care as your health needs increase.

Today, there are doctors who are known as concierge physicians. These physicians limit their practices to a given number of patients who pay an annual fee to have access to them whenever needed. The concierge physician is able to refer you to other specialists if and when needed. The cost for this service will vary in different parts of the country.

Health Care Availability

Wherever you live, an important factor for you to consider is the availability of health care. Are there doctors in the area you're considering who are willing to take you on as a patient if your only health insurance is Medicare? How accessible are these physicians to where you want to live? How close will you be to the nearest hospital? You certainly don't want to find yourself in an area where there's not much health care available. How will you be able to reach your physician's office? Is there public transportation readily available, or do you need to be driven to the location? For example, younger people might enjoy living in an area that is more isolated, but for you at this stage of your life, the appeal of the bucolic countryside might pale if there is little available in the way of health care if you experience a medical emergency.

PHYSICAL HEALTH

A good bit of what you're able to do and not do will depend on your physical health. Understanding both your strengths and weaknesses will help you develop a plan for yourself that's attainable and should contribute to keeping you healthy. If you haven't gotten around to having an annual physical since you retired now is a good time to make an appointment with your primary care physician for a full examination. As you age, regular visits to the doctor become more important, regardless of whether or not you believe you're having any new medical issues.

In addition to your annual physical, it's advisable to see your dentist and eye doctor at least once a year. As you know and are reminded of by the media with regularity, if there's a problem, the sooner it's identified, the sooner it can be treated, which in turn leads to a better outcome.

At this time in your life, it's important to monitor your health and medical appointments more carefully than you might have done when you were younger. You should keep a written record of the dates you saw your doctors to make sure your insurance covers these visits. For instance, currently, Medicare doesn't cover the cost of an annual physical if it takes place less than 365 days since your last physical.

MENTAL HEALTH

Your mental health can't be rigidly defined. It's not fixed, but rather fluctuates throughout your life based on your individual personality and life experiences. Retirement is a major life transition that affects the mental health of all retirees. For some, it's a positive experience and for others a negative one. It's difficult to predict with certainty how your mental health will be affected by your retirement.

By now, most of you have made the necessary adjustments to retired life. Some of you have done well, while others may still be struggling. This may be particularly true if you have left a job where you had ongoing responsibility for which you received a lot of recognition. It is difficult to go from a position of power to one without. You may find that you will take longer to adjust to this change in your life than you anticipated.

Just as you are mindful of your physical health in retirement, you also need to be mindful of your mental health. When you have your annual physical, make sure to share with your physician any and all emotional experiences you are having which are negatively impacting the quality of your life. Your physician will work with you to implement an appropriate course of action. This may include medication, a referral to a mental health professional or both.

Those of you who initially welcomed retirement may find that you're no longer as enthusiastic about it as you anticipated. Perhaps the honeymoon phase of euphoria and being able to control your own time you initially experienced might have changed to feelings of lethargy and uselessness. Regardless of where you have fallen on this continuum, you need to recognize that neither extreme is likely to last for any length of time. In all probability you'll level off somewhere in the middle.

Recognize it's common for recent retirees to experience major emotional swings between elation and depression, anxiety and optimism. The degree and frequency with which you experience these emotions will determine whether or not you should seek professional help. If you find yourself unable to enjoy most aspects of this new chapter in your life, do so.

Before leaving this topic, recognize that some retirees self-medicate in order to feel better. Alcohol is the most frequently used substance to deal with these issues. Its use and abuse will occur if unwanted destructive feelings are not addressed. Late onset addiction may occur when a woman is faced with a host of losses related to her retirement such as death of family members/friends, loss of identity tied to her career, and physical limitations. An additional complicating factor may be the negative effect of alcohol when mixed with necessary prescription drugs. Be aware that your partner may be vulnerable to these issues as well.

There are mental health professionals to help you sort out where you are and how best to get to a better place. There's no shame in not being ecstatic with retired life, but it would be a shame to lose these valuable years by ignoring what you are feeling. What is important is to seek whatever help you need to be fulfilled at this time in your life.

EXERCISE

An exercise routine is essential for all of us. We're assuming that now that you've completed your first full year of retirement, you've made a determination as to what sort of exercise program will best meet your needs and desires to stay active and fit. Whatever you've put in place, it's a good idea to review it annually with your physician to make sure that it's an appropriate program for you given your strengths and weaknesses. Your goal is to strike a balance between doing too much or not enough to maintain good physical condition. Even if you think you're in good physical shape, you need a clear understanding of what's reasonable so you are able to set realistic goals for yourself.

Many of you may have been exercising on a regular basis for years. If you're able to continue doing what you've been doing, by all means you should maintain that regimen. If prior to retiring you never exercised on a regular basis, we hope that by now you have put in place an exercise program. Remember you no longer can give the excuse of not having enough time!

There are fitness centers of one sort or another in just about every geographic area offering many classes and amenities. Perhaps you've started your exercise program in retirement by taking a class in yoga or pilates. Others of you may have looked wide-eyed at all the exercise machines available to improve your cardiovascular health, improve core strength, etc., and decided that rather than start on your own, you would sign up to work with a trainer. In addition to explaining what all the machines are capable of doing, the trainer can design a program that would be best for you. Some of you might have found that you wanted to continue working with the trainer on a weekly basis to keep you focused and provide structure to your workout. Others of you may prefer to work on your own. Again, the goal is to have selected a program that is right for you.

Perhaps going to a gym has never been your thing. That's not likely to have changed now that you're retired. Hopefully, you have determined what you could do at home either/or in your neighborhood to maintain your physical health. Alternatively, bike riding, walking or swimming may have appealed to you and you have made them part of your weekly routine. In addition to benefitting from your exercise regime, you might even be enjoying it!

Among other activities that have both a physical and emotional benefit is gardening. Not something one would necessarily imagine. However, some retirees have reported that although they may have never done any gardening in the past, gardening has always appealed to them. Now in retirement they decide to take it up. They usually start simply with fruits or vegetables that are easy to grow, for example tomatoes. Research confirms that working in the garden, which requires bending and moving, can contribute to better physical health. In addition, depending on where or with whom you might be trying this new activity, it might have a social advantage. One can garden in a single family home or town house, a terrace or even a community garden. If the latter, it often leads to new friendships with others that share your interest.

Remember to allow yourself to have no regrets if you have tried something that you thought you'd love only to find out that it wasn't what you thought it would be like at all. You should feel free to try something else that has always interested you that you never had the time to try before you retired. Don't be upset about having chosen something that didn't work out. Let yourself continue to explore new activities and options.

You and your partner may have planned to take a very ambitious trip that required specialized training in bicycling, hiking or climbing. This intense preparation might have provided you with much satisfaction relative to your being able to handle the demands of the trip, but keep in mind that it was a short-term endeavor. Remember to maintain your long-term exercise program that can be followed with regularity. Whatever you have put in place by this time should be based on your personal physical health. Perhaps going to a gym had never been your thing.

NUTRITION

In addition to your exercise regimen, you may have given more thought to your nutrition. At this point in our lives, you need to pay more attention to your dietary needs. In the past, you may have done a good job of balancing what you ate or might have been someone who grabbed fast food as you went about meeting your daily commitments.

Now that you have better control over your time and what you undertake on a daily basis, hopefully you've found some time to evaluate your eating habits and your diet in a way that you previously hadn't. When you meet with your physician for your annual physical, you will have an opportunity to discuss your nutrition with her. For instance, if she found that based on your bloodwork, you were deficient in a specific area, she probably would recommend that you eat more of certain foods and less of others. She also may have suggested a vitamin regimen. Depending on the issues identified, she even might have suggested that you consult a nutritionist to help you design a well-balanced diet for your specific needs.

Optional Paid/Volunteer Work For A Nonprofit

When you first retired, you might have taken some time to create lists of activities and endeavors that were important to you as well as those which you had no interest in doing. Headings such as family, friends, intellectual stimulation, home, travel, projects and exercise may have helped clarify for you how you wanted to spend your time. We hope you've been able to implement some of the things that were most important to you. Balance is always a good objective, but not so easy to define and obtain. It's all a component of ultimately determining what is right for you. Many researchers have reminded us that the best way to learn and grow is from our mistakes.

In this first year, many retirees decide that they want to spend some time making a contribution to others on either a paid or volunteer basis. The thought of working with a nonprofit may be very appealing. Most retirees take on these jobs on a part-time basis so they are in a position to explore other interests as well. These activities can provide you with intellectual stimulation while allowing you the opportunity to give back to society in a way that was unavailable to you in the past. One minor caveat—don't allow yourself to get enmeshed in any one activity, to the detriment of the total picture. You don't want to find yourself with the same pressures from the outside that you have left behind. Always be mindful of your physical and mental health and maintaining balance in everything you do.

Items To Consider As You Make Physical And Mental Adjustments In The First Year

- Monitor your physical health by seeing your medical professionals on a regular basis.

- Evaluate whether your current physicians will be able to meet your needs as you age.

- Whether you stay in place or relocate, make sure you're close to physicians, urgent care facilities/hospitals.

- Adopt an exercise routine that is appropriate for your physical condition.

- Maintaining a positive mental attitude is essential for an interesting and rewarding retirement.

- Consider working part-time for a nonprofit on a volunteer or paid basis.

- Seek medical guidance as to appropriate nutrition.

CATHERINE CHAPTER NINE:
PHYSICAL AND MENTAL ADJUSTMENTS IN THE FIRST YEAR

Was this real? She and Jordan were actually at the airport waiting for their flight to London. They hadn't taken a trip like this since their honeymoon. During the past few months they'd poured over travel books and with the help of a travel agent had created a trip that would allow them to spend some time in the three countries in which they knew they had roots. They recognized that they were just scratching the surface with this trip, but it was exhilarating to realize that they were actually doing something that had always been on their bucket lists.

Catherine had kept Jordan on her health insurance plan until he had applied for Medicare Parts A, B and D. At the same time, he'd also researched and selected a Medigap insurance policy which covered some of the costs not covered by Medicare.

Jordan's second career had resulted in his spending more time at the golf club they belonged to for so many years. Initially he'd started to play golf again because he had the time to do it and enjoyed the exercise. Now that he was involved in real estate, he thought the social contacts he made playing golf might help with potential real estate sales.

In the process, he was reminded that the club had a gym. He had always known this but never paid any attention in the past since his work kept him too busy to use it. He decided he should take advantage of this facility because he did believe that appearance was an important aspect of his work in the real estate market.

Jordan made an appointment with one of the club's personal trainers to help him develop an exercise program that would be right for him. In that first evaluation, he realized just how out of shape he was. They agreed that he would commit to a regular exercise program, including two days a week with the trainer.

In a short period of time, Catherine could see the change in Jordan's appearance and was inspired to make an appointment with his trainer for herself. The following Saturday she met with the trainer to do an assessment of her strengths and weaknesses and provide her with an exercise program that would meet her needs. The trainer pointed out that not only was exercise a good way to improve her overall health, but it also relieved stress. Catherine always knew that exercising regularly would be beneficial for both of them but previously hadn't done anything about it for herself.

On the nutrition side, during Jordan's moping around days she'd asked him to help her out by preparing some meals for them. Cooking never had been her favorite thing to do, but she encouraged him to look through her recipe box for recipes that appealed to him and that he thought he could manage to make. At the time she thought it would be good for him to have something to do to occupy his time, but to her surprise he had become involved in the meal preparation and begun to take an interest in the food they ate. He was totally committed to their eating more nutritious food. He even found out which farm stands were located in their area so that he could seasonally get the freshest fruits and vegetables available. She found that she actually enjoyed the meals he prepared. She and Ben joked with one another about the fact that neither one of them would have predicted that Jordan would take an interest in meal preparation.

Emily Chapter Nine:
Physical And Mental Adjustments In The First Year

Emily and Hank now had been living together for a year. They were discussing where they would like to live on a permanent basis and were about to begin an active search. They saw pluses and minuses to both a townhouse or an apartment. One thing they agreed on was that they'd like to be in some proximity to their current neighborhood, which was so convenient to everything.

Hank was still working full-time and she'd found a part-time job doing fundraising exclusively for one nonprofit. She enjoyed her work as well as her free time. Her health care needs were now covered by Medicare. She was pleased that she was able to continue to use her existing physicians and that their offices were located relatively close to their apartment. Since she was older than most of her doctors she felt no need to replace them. She'd even convinced Hank to change his primary care physician to the one she'd been using as she'd always appreciated her responsiveness to her when she needed her.

She and Hank had agreed that she should continue to meet with Shelley on an annual basis. This past year Hank had gone with her so they could discuss their financial situation together.

Her friendship with her yoga friend Carla had expanded to the point where they now did things together as couples as well as just the women. The men had much in common. Last fall they'd even taken a three-day weekend trip to the Outer Banks. She never would have believed that she could establish a new friendship that would become as meaningful to her as her existing female friends.

Emily and Hank made a joint decision that they really needed to do something about an exercise program other than taking an occasional walk. Emily took it upon herself to see what her fitness center had to offer. They'd always both enjoyed riding bikes and decided that maybe they should commit to a spinning class on Saturday mornings. The class was held in the late morning so they still would have time for their leisurely breakfast and newspaper reading before they had to get ready to leave. After class they could stay and use some of the machines available at the gym. They also promised themselves that when the weather was good they would make an effort to go for a three-mile bike ride in the park near where they lived. They even talked about taking a biking trip in the future. "Not yet," she thought.

As to their diet and nutrition, they both watched what they ate in terms of salt intake and fatty foods. They were cognizant of how foods impacted their cholesterol levels and were guided accordingly. On Sundays they made a list of the meals they were going to eat at home in the coming week and created a shopping list. They even would agree on the dinner menus for the times they ate at home. Hank liked to putter around in the kitchen and participate in the food preparation. She found having him in the kitchen with her so rewarding. They usually ate out two to three times a week as well in local restaurants. Doug never stepped foot in the kitchen other than to grab a drink from the fridge or get a snack. This was a different relationship—one she really valued.

Perhaps the biggest change had taken place with Carter. He and Louise were getting serious and talking about moving in together within the next year. Hank truly enjoyed the time he spent with Carter and had taken him to several ball games. He also frequently included Carter when he and his son, Harvey, were going to some sporting event. Olivia, Hank's granddaughter, really looked up to Carter in terms of what he was able to contribute to her soccer team as an assistant coach. That in turn made Carter feel better about himself.

Emily couldn't help but wonder how different Carter's life might have been if his father had given him any time or suggested that he approved of him on any level. She knew that it wasn't productive to revisit the past. What mattered now was how best to move forward. She couldn't stop being amazed at how things had turned out.

Emily remembered how devastated she'd been when Doug first asked her for a divorce. Back then, she would have done anything to salvage the marriage. What had been wrong with her? She and Doug never had a shared relationship. It was always what Doug wanted or needed. She would have missed so much if they had stayed together. Maybe she should thank him!

MELISSA CHAPTER NINE:
PHYSICAL AND MENTAL ADJUSTMENTS IN THE FIRST YEAR

Melissa recognized how much she'd come to value the time she and David spent in Sarasota. As she sat in a rocking chair on their balcony, she loved to feel the sun on her face and think to herself how lucky she was to be warm in February.

After renting the apartment for a year, she and David had decided to buy it. The winters in Florida had benefitted both of them. It had taken her some time to get past feeling guilty about being in Florida while Hannah and Chris had to deal with Michigan winters. She was there now. Actually, their present arrangement allowed them to have the best of both worlds. They now spent about six months in Florida and the rest of the year in their townhouse in Bloomfield Hills.

David continued to play golf on a regular basis and as a result was looking more fit. He said he was feeling better than he had in years. She'd actually started doing some exercise as well. One of the women she knew from Detroit who had moved down here had asked her to take a water aerobics class with her. Melissa wasn't sure she wanted anyone to see her in a bathing suit, but her friend assured her that there was no reason to be concerned. Reluctantly, she agreed to try it. To her surprise, she did find it to be fun. After the first class she realized she had many muscle groups that hadn't been used in years. She did ache but decided not to quit because she really enjoyed the other women in the class. It didn't seem like such a chore when they were doing it together.

She'd always enjoyed cooking, but in Florida she really took advantage of the fresh fruits and vegetables which were in plentiful supply. There was a farmer's market open on Saturday mornings which she enjoyed going to on a regular basis. As a result, they just seemed to eat more healthy foods. She expanded her food preparation repertoire to include interesting salads and fish—something they rarely ate when they lived in Michigan.

They'd debated about what to do with their medical care. They both were enrolled in Medicare, so there were no issues with regard to coverage, but what to do about changing physicians was a concern when they were in Florida. They really had benefitted from talking to Jane and Bill Jamieson, their friends from Michigan, who'd relocated to Sarasota earlier than they had. Bill had some issues with his heart that motivated them to investigate local doctors. After some trial and error, they'd found a cardiologist and internist who seemed to meet their needs. Jane and Bill suggested that Melissa and David make an appointment to meet these doctors and see what they thought. They agreed that David should establish a relationship with a cardiologist in Sarasota prior to needing one. This sounded like a good plan.

The Jamiesons told them that last year Bill had ended up in the hospital with the flu and was pleased with the treatment he'd received there. This was reassuring to David and Melissa, since the hospital was located only a couple of miles from their apartment. They also mentioned that they had considered signing up with a concierge doctor. Melissa and David didn't think they needed that right now, but they wanted to have doctors who were familiar with their medical histories in case anything happened to them when they were in Florida. These doctors wouldn't replace their Detroit doctors but could work collaboratively with them.

Prior to David's retirement, Melissa had worried about David being at loose ends when he was retired and would want to spend all his free time with her. This would have been a big adjustment for her, since she was used to having her own life which she had built over the years. Not only was caring for family important to her but so were her volunteer activities with the church and time with her female friends.

She was pleasantly surprised that David seemed to find things he liked to do besides golf. He had gotten involved with the local Corvette club. He always had been interested in cars because of his job and even had an antique Corvette. He hadn't been able to spend much time with this hobby, but now that he was retired he joined the local club and went to regular meetings.

In fact, Melissa found that she and David had grown closer since they had retired. In addition to pursuing separate activities they found that there were things they liked to do together. They'd both developed an interest in learning more about the history of Sarasota. They'd designated one day a week for them to spend exploring their surroundings or attending a lecture that expanded their knowledge of the area in which they now lived. They'd learned so much and truly enjoyed their mini road trips together.

Victoria Chapter Nine:
Physical And Mental Adjustments In The First Year

Victoria realized that her life had changed in some areas since she'd retired, but there still were similarities to the life she led while working. Last week she'd had her annual appointment with Dr. Ross. He found her to be in good shape. They'd discussed the work she'd been doing with some of his patients. Following the discussion they'd had just prior to her full retirement, she'd indicated to him that she would welcome the opportunity to work with any of his patients he felt would benefit from some one-on-one support.

In the past year she'd spent time with four of his patients. It had been an unbelievably rewarding experience. She could relate to these women on such a personal level. All of them had been younger than she was by at least ten years but it didn't seem to matter. They welcomed all she had to share based on her experience. She understood their fears and knew how to help. She spent time doing things with them, occasionally accompanying them to treatments and cooking with them.

Dr. Ross had asked her to review with them her good eating habits. He said he was often appalled at what poor dietary habits some of his patients had. She'd copied some of her favorite, yet easy-to-prepare recipes, and put them in a small notebook for these women. She was amazed at how grateful they all were for her support. With two of the women, their spouses thanked her profusely, telling her how much her positive attitude had helped them.

Victoria shared with Dr. Ross that an unanticipated outgrowth of her putting some recipes together for a few of his patients was her decision to create a garden in her own backyard. Why buy tomatoes when she might be able to grow them, to say nothing of herbs? She'd started with a few different types of plants: namely tomatoes, beans and herbs, but soon expanded to other vegetables. She had read that gardening tended to benefit retirees' health but had never thought about it for herself. Somewhat to her surprise, she'd found that she truly enjoyed working with the earth. It sounded silly, she thought, but there was something grounding about feeling the earth on her hands. Who would have thought, she told him, that in an effort to help others, I would help myself.

She'd maintained and expanded her physical fitness activity. She had a weekly routine. She made a point of running outdoors at least three times per week, weather permitting. As a retired professor, she was able to use the university gym if it wasn't being used for classes, games or physical instruction. As a result, she would try to get to the gym three times a week to use some of the machines they had to strengthen her core muscles, arms and abs. She did allow herself at least one day a week off. It was an ambitious routine, but she felt so much better physically and mentally if she maintained it. She was even giving some thought to training for a mini marathon.

Victoria had rented her basement apartment to a female professor who was new to the university and wanted an apartment for the first year. Their personalities complimented each other, and despite their age difference, they enjoyed shared activities. In addition, Victoria was a good sounding board for the woman with regard to the workings of the university. She found herself assuming the role of a mentor, which she found rewarding. They were mutually satisfied with this arrangement. Her cat, Sandy, had also benefitted from the rental of the apartment. Now when Victoria went to San Francisco, she didn't have to get one of her friends to take care of him. He could stay in his home and continue with all his usual patterns.

CHAPTER TEN

Investment
and Estate Planning

*E*arlier in your life, you and/or your partner may have handled your own investments and been somewhat casual about your estate planning. Now, at this point, you can't afford that luxury. Retirement provides an ideal time to review your investments and estate plan (assuming you have one) and to make appropriate changes as warranted. There are many helpful books on both investment and estate planning (a few of which we've listed in our resource section), but in this chapter we've provided some basic guidelines for you to consider.

Be Involved In Planning Your Future Financial Life
In the past, you might have delegated the handling of financial affairs to your partner. Even if you were working outside the home, you had your hands full also running your household as well as social activities. If you could delegate anything to someone else to do, such as

managing the investments, you might have done so. According to a UBS Global Wealth Management report released in 2017, a majority of married women—56 percent—still leave major investing and financial planning decisions to their partner.

However, as we consistently have pointed out, statistically, women outlive men, so there is a good chance that sometime in the future, you'll have the primary responsibility for managing your finances. Now that you have more time to be involved in this important activity, you should participate. You don't have to become a professional investment advisor, but you do need to understand the basic terms and help to make decisions that affect your future. It's okay to delegate but not to abdicate. If you're single, you've had to be responsible for your financial life in the past, but now it's more important than ever.

Assemble A Team Of Trustworthy And Knowledgeable Advisors

Regretfully, as you grow older, you may not be able to make financial decisions as well as you did when you were younger. Now is the time to line up advisors who can provide you with objective, knowledgeable advice based on their experience. As time goes by, you'll need to rely on your financial advisors more to help you manage your investments and make good decisions based on current laws and market conditions. This team would include a financial planner, lawyer, accountant and an insurance agent. You'll have to pay for this advice, but we believe compensating these experts is one of the best investments you can make to insure a secure retirement.

If you already have advisors, determine if they are experienced in working with clients such as yourself, in this new chapter of your life. If you don't have advisors, we suggest you find ones who have this expertise. Their role will be to advise you for the rest of your life. We recommend you consult them for any major financial decision you're contemplating making.

INVESTMENT PLANNING

ESTABLISH YOUR LONG-TERM FINANCIAL GOALS

Your primary financial goal is to have sufficient income to cover your expenses for your lifetime. However, you may fall into the group of people who want to cash their last check when they die (very hard to achieve with any certainty). Alternatively, it may be important to you to make sure there is money left to leave to your heirs and/or charities. If you have a partner, you need to make sure you agree on your goals or make some kind of compromise. Your professional advisors can help you with this process.

ASSESS YOUR RISK TOLERANCE

Your risk tolerance reflects your emotional ability to handle losses without flinching or acting without sufficient thought. Your risk tolerance may have been formed when you were a child by your parents' experiences or attitudes, or it may be attributed to your experience in your adult life, such as the decline of the stock market in 2008. Again, if you have a partner, it is not unusual for your risk tolerance/ capacity to differ. If so, you need to talk this over in order to reach some kind of consensus.

Now that you're retired, it's likely your predictable income is lower than it was earlier in your life. You're no longer in the accumulation phase of your life, but rather in the withdrawal mode. Therefore, you may not be comfortable taking as much risk with your investments.

It's important to convey to your financial advisor how much risk you are comfortable taking at this stage of your life.

WOMEN ARE GOOD INVESTORS

In May 2017, Fidelity Investments published a study of male and female investors. The bottom line was that females actually did better than men. Interestingly enough, these findings were confirmed by a study by Neil Stewart, a professor at Warwick Business School in the United Kingdom, published in November 2018. Both these studies attributed this outperformance to several factors:

1. Women are less inclined to take risk and do research before investing.
2. They are more patient and take a longer-term view then men.
3. They tend to buy and hold rather than try to time the market,
4. They look at life goals versus focusing on investment performance alone.

ASSET ALLOCATION FOR A RETIREE

Asset allocation is a fancy way of saying how your investments should be divided between cash, bonds, stocks and other kinds of investments. The purpose of asset allocation is to apportion your investments in such a way that you meet your investment goals and at the same time minimize the effects of periodic market fluctuations to the degree possible. Your asset allocation depends on your goals, your life expectancy as well as your risk tolerance.

Asset allocation is based on the fact that different kinds of investments perform well at different times. For instance, common stocks might do better than bonds one year and the reverse the following year. It's difficult to predict which kind of investment will do the best in a particular year.

In order to stabilize your portfolio over time, experts recommend you have a balance between different kinds of investments. The simplest version of asset allocation would be to have a balance between stocks and bonds. One frequently used formula for retirees has been to invest 40 percent bonds and 60 percent stocks.

In today's world, asset allocation models have become more complex. Typically, advisors recommend investing a certain percentage in the following kinds of investments: cash/bonds, stocks of United States companies, stocks of international companies and alternative investments (such as real estate investment trusts).

DON'T TRY TO TIME THE MARKET

If you're invested in good quality stocks and bonds, you should hold onto them. This is sometimes easier said than done. If you have an ample cash reserve and an advisor to guide you through the inevitable turbulent times, you should be able to weather the storm successfully.

To illustrate this point, if you invested $10,000 in 2003 in the S & P Index with dividends reinvested by the end of 2018, your nest egg would be worth a little over $30,000. If you had missed the ten best days in the stock market during that time period, it would be worth about half that amount—$15,000. If you had missed the twenty best days, you would be back to your original investment of $10,000 (source: Putnam Investments).

TAX PLANNING

While you should be aware of the tax implications of making changes in your portfolio, we don't believe that paying taxes should prevent you from making changes in your investments. If your advisor recommends a sale of an investment where the fundamentals have changed, there is a good reason for this recommendation. Even if the sale means you will pay taxes on the capital gain, you should follow this advice. Otherwise, if you delay selling, ultimately you may find yourself with a loss instead of a gain.

Beware Of Fraudulent Schemes

If someone you don't know approaches you with an investment idea, be cautious. Don't be too quick to invest. Beware of individuals who offer you guarantees of spectacular profits in a short time frame without risk. When something sounds too good to be true it probably is.

In 2018 the Federal Trade Commission received nearly 3 million complaints. These losses totaled $1.48 billion, which was up 38 percent from the prior year. We would suggest there are others who have been defrauded who are too embarrassed to admit they have been taken!

These con artists particularly prey on single older women whom they assume are more susceptible to being deceived and are lonely. Some have even taken advantage of online dating by first gaining your trust and then asking for a loan.

Red flags are when someone asks for your bank account/credit account information or your Social Security number, requests you to wire money, pressures you to make an immediate decision, and discourages you from asking advice about the investment from an impartial third party.

The adage "there is no such thing as a free lunch" is true. You may be invited to a "free" lunch or dinner where you will listen to an "educational" lecture about a surefire investment. While this session might be perfectly legitimate, make sure you investigate further before making a decision and always request written information about the proposed investment. If you do invest, don't invest more than you can afford to lose.

REVIEW YOUR FINANCIAL SITUATION ANNUALLY

The job of planning for retirement never ends. Tax laws change, investment choices change and your personal circumstances change. Therefore, it's important to review your financial situation at least annually to make sure your income is covering your expenses and to determine if you should reposition your investments and/or make changes.

ESTATE PLANNING

The most important reason to have an estate plan is to make sure that your assets are distributed as you would like. If you die without a will, the laws of your state will dictate where your assets go. This may not be as you wish. To create your estate planning documents, we strongly recommend you consult with an estate planning lawyer in the state in which you are domiciled (this is the technical term for your legal residence).

The Tax Cuts and Jobs Act of 2017 eliminated federal estate taxes for everyone whose estates are less than $11.58 million (as of 2020). Since most people don't have assets of this magnitude, you may think this law eliminates your need for estate planning. However, this exemption expires at the end of 2025. At the beginning of 2026, the estate exemption declines to $5 million, adjusted for inflation. These laws could be changed legislatively at any time. In addition, some states impose their own estate tax and/or an inheritance tax on their residents.

ESTATE PLANNING DOCUMENTS

WILL

The most basic document is the **will**. Your will is a legal document that describes how your estate assets are to be divided among your heirs. In this document you name a personal representative to carry out the terms of the will. It is important to get the consent of your personal representative prior to naming her. If she's concerned about assuming this responsibility, recommend she work with the lawyer who created the estate plan. Stipulate in this document that the expense of settling the estate be paid from the estate assets.

DURABLE POWERS OF ATTORNEY (DPOA)

These **DPOA**s appoint a person to act on your behalf should you be traveling or unable to act for yourself due to physical or cognitive disability.

You should have two durable powers of attorney, one to handle your financial affairs and the other to cover your health care directives. You might give two different people these powers of attorney or have one person assume both responsibilities.

LIVING WILL/AN ADVANCE MEDICAL DIRECTIVE

A living will is different from a health power of attorney. A living will specifies your wishes to withhold or withdraw treatment if you're a candidate for life support and are considered terminal. In some states the health care power of attorney and the living will are combined into one document **called an advance medical directive.**

$\mathcal{L}$IVING $\mathcal{T}$RUST

Finally, many people choose to have a **living trust** document. This is a written agreement that's established while you're alive. Typically, you name yourself as the trustee and someone else as the successor trustee if you are unable to act for yourself. As with the will, make sure to get the agreement of the person you have appointed to be your trustee. Living trusts are popular since assets held in a living trust don't go through probate, aren't a matter of public record (unlike assets controlled by the will), and are less likely to be challenged.

If you do have a living trust, make sure you transfer your investment and bank accounts into the name of the trust. This trust won't achieve your objectives if your assets aren't titled in the trust name.

Recently, the question of disposition of digital data has come up. Many states have enacted the Revised Uniform Fiduciary Access to Digital Assets Act (RUFADAA). This law was developed to provide executors and attorneys with a legal path to manage the digital assets of deceased or incapacitated people. This document is made part of your other legal documents.

$\mathcal{D}$ISTRIBUTION $\mathcal{O}$F $\mathcal{A}$SSETS $\mathcal{N}$OT $\mathcal{C}$OVERED $\mathcal{B}$Y $\mathcal{T}$HE $\mathcal{W}$ILL

You may be surprised to learn that your will doesn't cover all your assets. Your retirement accounts and insurance policies have their own beneficiary designation. You should have a named beneficiary and successor beneficiary for each of your retirement accounts. Periodically check with the relevant entities and ask them to provide this information in writing for your records.

For personal property, it's advisable for you to prepare a letter of instruction that outlines who gets which pieces of jewelry, paintings or other personal items. Make sure your personal representative and lawyer have a copy of this letter, since such a letter can prevent family squabbles after you die.

How To Make The Estate Settlement Process Easier For Your Family

Ideally, you should have a family meeting and explain what your plans are for the disposition of your estate. If you are reluctant to reveal the amounts of money involved, you can talk in general terms.

If you haven't already done so, we suggest you set up a fireproof file cabinet in which you will keep all your important papers. This would include your estate planning documents, the location and key for your safety deposit box, Social Security numbers, birth, marriage and divorce certificates, list of your financial institutions, pensions, life insurance and annuities, tax returns, deeds to property and cemetery plots, passports, vehicle titles and registrations. You also should have a list of the names and contact information for your financial advisor, lawyer, and accountant. It's important that your personal representative knows the password to your computer—in fact all your passwords. It also would be helpful to have a list of your credit cards as well as which bills should be paid when.

Most investment firms offer some system which can digitally store some or all this information for you. Whatever you do, make sure your personal representative and family members know where these records are kept.

When allocating your assets to your heirs, it's recommended to use percentages rather than dollar amounts. Otherwise, when you die, you might not have sufficient money to satisfy the dollar amounts you have specified. By using percentages, you avoid this pitfall.

Some people think to avoid playing favorites they should name all their children as personal representatives for their estate. This can cause real havoc when settling the estate. We recommend you appoint one person who is the most logical to assume this task. Ideally, this person lives geographically near you, understands your family dynamics and will be responsible in distributing the assets.

One Final Note

You may want to take estate planning a step further and think ahead to the type of funeral or memorial service you may want.

For example, do you want a religious or non-religious memorial service? Are there individuals you would like to speak at this ceremony? Who will be the pallbearers? Where do you want the ceremony to take place? Do you want to be cremated or buried in a coffin (if so, what kind)? Do you want your body/organs donated to science? Where do you want to be buried? Do you have a cemetery plot?

The more you can preplan, the easier it will be for your survivors. You might consider prepaying for your funeral and burial arrangements. Having to make these decisions without previous guidance from you can be very stressful for the family.

ITEMS TO CONSIDER WHEN MANAGING YOUR INVESTMENTS AND MAKING YOUR ESTATE PLANS

- Be involved in the investment management process.

- Assemble a good team of advisors.

- List your short- and long-term financial goals

- Acknowledge your risk tolerance and share with your advisor.

- Understand need for balance between different kinds of investments.

- Buy good quality investments and hold them.

- Be aware of tax consequences of investment changes and withdrawal programs.

- Beware of doing business with strangers.

- Review your financial situation annually and make necessary adjustments.

- Make sure your estate planning documents are up to date and review periodically.

- Inform your family of your estate plans.

- Set up a fireproof file cabinet to house all your financial records.

- Consider preplanning for your demise.

CATHERINE CHAPTER TEN:
INVESTMENT AND ESTATE PLANNING

Catherine was pleased that she and Jordan were much more aware of their financial situation than they'd ever been. They frequently acknowledged that although Jordan's losing his job was traumatic for both of them, it did force them to look at their financial situation and plan for their retirement. She wondered what would have happened to them if they'd continued to be so casual about their future.

They'd followed Joe's advice and now were tracking their expenses on a computer program. They even were able to give their accountant their tax information in a timely fashion as opposed to the last minute rush they'd experienced in the past.

Previously, Catherine hadn't attended the semiannual retirement plan meetings the law firm provided for the partners. At these meetings a representative of the managing investment firm would review the performance of the funds included in their 401(k) plan. She now was going to these meetings and actually found she was interested in the information provided.

She provided Joe with regular statements of her retirement plan. He would combine the statements for Jordan's IRA, their joint investments and her 401(k) so they could look at everything as a total picture. Then he helped her choose the funds that fit into their total asset allocation. Based on their risk tolerance profiles, he had selected "moderate growth" as their investment objective.

Since Jordan was making money, not only were they able to avoid withdrawing any money from his retirement plan, he was contributing to a new retirement account in his name. In a recent meeting, Joe had put together a new scenario, one that reflected both of them continuing to work until age 70 and contributing the maximum to their respective retirement plans. Based on his projections, it appeared that if they wanted to stop working at that time they could afford to do so. Although one or both of them might choose to continue to work longer, it was reassuring to know they didn't have to do so. You couldn't predict when health issues might intervene!

They sat down with James and Amanda and recommended strongly to them that they should pay attention to their own financial situations. They admitted to their children that they had not paid as much attention to their finances as they should have and they wanted to make sure that the children avoided making the same mistake.

Joe had agreed to meet with James and Amanda individually. In both cases he advised them to pay attention to their budgets. Since James was eligible to contribute to a 401(k) plan at work, Joe encouraged him to contribute the maximum he could, particularly since James' firm matched his contribution up to a certain level. Joe reviewed James' investment choices in the retirement plan and helped him select ones that he thought were appropriate for him in view of his risk tolerance. Joe also advised him that his budget should include a regular savings program where he could start accumulating a cash reserve. Although Amanda was still in law school, he suggested she track her expenses as well, so that when she started working, she would be aware of her financial situation. This would stand her in good stead.

Investment and Estate Planning

Since estate planning was Catherine's area of expertise, she and Jordan had updated all their legal documents. They were each other's personal representative. They'd selected Amanda as their successor personal representative, since she would be the lawyer in the family. As for the health care power of attorney, they asked James to take over that responsibility. They were very definite as to their end-of-life wishes, which they shared with their children.

All in all, Catherine thought they were in great shape and the future looked bright.

Emily Chapter Ten:
Investment And Estate Planning

Since Emily had been living on her own for more than ten years, she found it took a little time to adjust to living with someone full-time. However, Hank was so easy going, it didn't take that long for them to settle into a good routine. She thought Hank's former wife might create some problems for them, but that didn't materialize. Now that Hank no longer had to pay alimony, they didn't have much contact, except for occasional discussions about Hank's granddaughters.

The other night Hank had taken her to dinner at their favorite restaurant. At dinner, he brought up the subject of their future living arrangements. Since their lease was due to expire soon, he thought they should start looking for something to buy. He sort of talked around the subject and then finally blurted out—"Will you marry me?" Emily had thought about marriage, but was old-fashioned enough that she wasn't going to be the one to introduce the subject. She was thrilled he'd asked her in this manner and immediately accepted.

Originally Hank had thought that their moving to a townhouse would be a good idea but he'd become accustomed to the ease of apartment living. They had looked at both townhouses and apartments. Whatever they bought, they knew they needed more space than the 1500 square feet they currently had. After looking for awhile they found the perfect place. It was a 2400 square-foot spacious apartment with three bedrooms and 3.5 baths. It was reasonably priced. If they put 20 percent down, the payments, including the condo fee, would be affordable. Hank suggested they continue their current arrangement. She could pay for one third of the down payment and one third of the monthly payments and she would own one third of the apartment.

Emily had cleared $600,000 from the sale of her house. She didn't have to use much of the proceeds to supplement her living expenses, particularly once she had started working as a fundraiser for the nonprofit. She still had $550,000 left from the house sale and hadn't had to tap into her retirement funds.

Emily was receiving half of Doug's Social Security income, which she realized she'd have to give up if she married Hank before he started collecting his Social Security income when he turned 70, which was two years away. At that time, she could receive half of Hank's Social Security income. Emily smiled to herself. Only a few years ago it wouldn't have occurred to her to consider the financial side of marriage. Waiting two more years to get married was a small price to pay for the added retirement income, and she was sure Hank would agree.

Before making an offer to buy the apartment, they had met with Shelley to review their financial situation. During the last couple of years Emily had kept much better records and knew exactly what their expenses were, so Shelley had no trouble entering them into the computer. She agreed that the apartment purchase seemed to fit well into their budget and that the mortgage interest and real estate taxes would provide them with deductions they didn't previously have.

As part of their meeting Shelley asked them how long they intended to continue to work. Although both of them had planned to stop working when they turned 70, they were having second thoughts. They might want to work longer. Emily really liked the work she was doing and found it very rewarding to be able to raise money to help families of cancer victims. Since she was working part-time she still had time to do other things as well. As long as she was healthy and the nonprofit had no issues with her age, she couldn't see any reason to stop working. Besides, she liked having the extra money.

Hank had a similar situation. Since he was a partner in the firm, he wasn't required to retire at a certain age. He had talked to his partners about not taking any new clients and only servicing his current ones, and they seemed amenable to that idea. As long as he was willing to keep current on the latest tax laws, he could continue to work at the firm. In fact, he could do a lot of the work from home. It seemed the idea of phased in retirement was gaining traction in many professions. They both realized that they were fortunate that they could make these choices rather than working for a big corporation which would require them to stop working at a certain age.

Shelley brought up the topic of estate planning. The last documents Emily had were prepared after her divorce 12 years earlier. Emily realized it was important that she make sure Carter was protected. Jill was in much better financial shape than Carter, and seemed to have a stable marriage. Shelley suggested that she schedule an appointment with an estate planning lawyer to set up a trust so Carter would have a source of income should something happen to Emily. That seemed like a good idea to Emily.

Hank and she discussed it and decided that when they got married, they would arrange their affairs so that Emily's children would inherit her assets and Hank's family would inherit his. They agreed with Shelley that they needed to get all their legal documents reviewed by an estate planning lawyer sooner rather than later. When they got married they could have them updated again. Shelley gave them the name of some lawyers she worked with and they agreed to meet with one soon.

Melissa Chapter Ten:
Investment And Estate Planning

Melissa and David had settled into a routine, dividing their time between their two residences. As time went on they found they were spending more time in Florida, but they were always glad to return to Michigan during the summer. Although they missed seeing their children and grandchildren all the time, the warm weather in Florida compensated. Also, both Hannah and Chris and their children came down to see them at least once a year. They even were able to get Matthew and Terry to come to Florida as well. Somehow they found visiting them in Sarasota more appealing than Detroit!

Their accountant, Charles, had pointed out to them the tax advantages of becoming Florida residents. If they were domiciled in Florida, they would no longer have to pay Michigan income tax. The sales tax was about the same in both states. The real estate tax was actually higher in Michigan than Florida. However, if your Florida home was right on the water, the taxes could be higher. He recommended that they locate an estate planning lawyer in Sarasota and find out what they needed to do to become official residents of Florida.

When talking to their friends from Michigan, they found that most of them had become Florida residents. In checking with them, one estate planning lawyer's name "Martin McPherson" kept coming up and so they had made an appointment to see him. At their meeting, he provided them with a brochure which outlined all the steps they needed to take to become "domiciled" in Florida.

In order for them to proceed with becoming official Florida residents, they needed to have their legal papers redrafted to reflect Florida law. Actually, it had been a number of years since they had reviewed their estate plan, so this gave them a good opportunity to make much needed changes, such as providing for their grandchildren.

It was obvious that a lot of work was involved in becoming Florida residents, but it certainly seemed worthwhile. It felt a little strange to think about not paying Michigan any more taxes after living there all their lives, but on the other hand, they had paid taxes to Michigan for all their working years!

Martin suggested as part of establishing Florida residency, they consider having their other financial advisors based in Florida. Having their estate documents prepared in Florida was a good first step but they might want to use a local accountant and even financial advisor.

David had used Charles as their accountant as long as he and Melissa had been married, but since he was about their age, there was a good chance he might be retiring soon. Perhaps it was time to make a change. He would talk to him about this the next time they were home.

As for replacing his financial advisor, David was really happy with his financial advisor, Ted Johnson, who was relatively young, but had worked at a well-established regional investment firm for over ten years. In fact, Ted had other clients who were "snowbirds" and he came down to Sarasota once a year to meet with them. So, no need to make a change there.

Prior to leaving for Florida in the winter David and Melissa had a meeting with Ted to review their investments. Previously

Melissa had been relatively passive at these meetings, but now she wanted to understand their financial situation better so she asked several questions. Ted had given them a report about the investment portfolio he managed for them. He pointed out that since they had a pension providing them with regular income, they didn't need to own as many bonds in the portfolio as they would if they didn't have this monthly income. However Ted wasn't comfortable with having such a large percentage (30 percent) invested in David's company stock which he had accumulated over the years. While he agreed that it was a good company, he thought having such a large percentage of their portfolio in one stock was risky. Although he realized that selling this stock would involve their paying capital gains taxes, he suggested instead that they reduce their position gradually over a period of time to reduce the tax bite. In the past, David thought selling the stock would be disloyal to his employer, but now that he was retired he could see that Ted's suggestion to lighten up on the position in stages made sense, and he agreed to follow it.

When he first retired, David had left his 401(k) assets invested with his company. Ted told him that he could roll the plan over into a self-directed IRA. This would provide him with a wider range of investment choices, and he and Melissa would have the advantage of having all his investments in one place, which would make it easier for them to follow. This appealed to Melissa. Since he'd been pleased with the investment results Ted had achieved with their personal investments, David asked Ted to give him the paperwork he needed to make this change

During one of their Sunday brunch talks, Melissa told David that she thought it might be a good idea to have a family meeting this summer with the children. At this meeting they could review their estate plan with all of them. They didn't have to tell them how much money was involved but they could explain what they had arranged. Distributing their estate would be pretty simple, since they expected to divide the assets equally between the three children, although they were going to leave approximately $10,000 outright to each of the four grandchildren as well as to three of their favorite charities. They'd made each other the personal representative for their wills as well as health and financial powers of attorney. In case either of them wasn't able to serve, they had designated Hannah as their personal representative, since she was the closest to them geographically. If she was unable to serve, they'd named Chris as their successor trustee.

David had put together one set of legal and financial documents, which he kept in a fireproof file. He made a duplicate copy to keep in Florida. He also included a list of people to contact if anything happened to either of them. They would make sure both Hannah and Chris knew where these files were kept in Florida and Michigan should access be needed.

VICTORIA CHAPTER TEN:
INVESTMENT AND ESTATE PLANNING

Victoria was quite satisfied with her current life. She was in relatively good health due to her exercise routine and diet habits. The income from her retirement plan, her Social Security income and the apartment rental seemed to more than cover her financial needs. The renovation of the basement, her kitchen and her bathrooms had depleted her inherited portfolio somewhat, but due to John's wise advice and a strong stock market, it had moved back up to its original value and was paying her some income.

When John had first started helping Victoria with her retirement planning, he'd asked her to fill out a risk tolerance questionnaire. The results indicated that on a scale of 1 to 100, she was a 45, which indicated that she wasn't willing to take a lot of risk with her investments. Neither of them was very surprised with these results. Based on this profile, as well as his conversation with her, he invested her portfolio conservatively investing about 40 percent in bonds and 60 percent in stocks.

Because he was concerned about rising interest rates, which make bond prices go down, he had bought relatively short-term bonds. He further explained the stocks were of established companies which had a history of consistently rising earnings and dividends. He had included some international companies as well as ones based in the United States. He called it a "you can sleep at night" portfolio which should enable her not to worry about the stock market when it declined in value from time to time as it was bound to do. Since she retired she'd met with John periodically to review her investments and update him on any changes in her life. She'd come to really appreciate John's advice, which had worked so well for her over the years.

In addition to her investments, Victoria had accumulated a travel fund. She'd built it up over the years so that when she wanted to spend money on a trip which exceeded her regular monthly expenses she could tap into this fund. She found that having this cash reserve as well as her retirement income enabled her not to worry about the vicissitudes of the stock market.

Unfortunately, Victoria's mother had died a few months ago. As a family they were grateful that her mother didn't experience a prolonged illness but died in her sleep. Victoria was pleased that during the last couple of years of her mother's life she'd been able to spend more time with her and felt she had gotten to know and appreciate her more as an adult. She also felt good about having made it possible for her mother to spend more time with her grandchildren.

Her mother had put her assets in a living trust, and Victoria was the trustee. As a result, her estate didn't need to go through probate, which saved them time and money. Victoria appreciated the fact that her mother's legal documents were all in order and settling her estate was relatively easy. She had provided that each of her four grandchildren would get $7,500, two charities would receive $15,000 each and the rest would be divided among her three children. She'd even written a letter of instructions outlining who should get which of her personal possessions. This included some pieces of jewelry and paintings.

Her mother had also arranged and prepaid for her cremation. It was important to her mother that the family have a memorial service for her as opposed to a funeral. She felt that a memorial service provided an opportunity for family members and friends to get together and remember her with appreciation and some humor.

Victoria was impressed at how organized her mother was in preparing for her own demise. Her mother had given her children the gift of attempting to anticipate any problem that might arise and addressing it before she died. They all appreciated their mother's thoughtfulness.

Her mother's death motivated Victoria to review her own legal documents, which she realized should be updated. She was fortunate that, after some discussion, her sister, Winnie, had agreed to be her personal representative as well as assume her power of attorney for her health and financial issues. Victoria convinced her that she was the logical person for her to appoint. She'd made it clear it shouldn't require that much time for her to settle the estate. She should consult the law firm for assistance in settling the estate and the legal fees should be paid from her estate.

CHAPTER ELEVEN

People Who Can Help You

*T*here's no reason for you to go it alone in this new phase in your life. There are many people who can assist you through your financial, physical and mental transition. This chapter provides a brief description of these professionals, including their qualifications and their fee structures.

Any advisor you select should be knowledgeable, ethical, empathetic and experienced. When looking for a specific advisor, ask your existing professional advisors to recommend someone. Your friends might also suggest someone with whom they have worked satisfactorily. Find out the experts' fee structure and what services will be provided before you sign any agreements or make a payment.

FINANCIAL PROFESSIONALS

We think the primary financial professionals who can assist you with your retirement planning are your financial planner, lawyer and accountant. In addition, there are several others who can advise you on specific aspects of your retirement.

Financial Planners

The primary goal of a financial planner is to review your overall financial situation and make specific recommendations to help you decide how your assets can provide you with adequate retirement income, taking into consideration your risk tolerance and tax situation.

The best-known credential in the financial planning profession is the CERTIFIED FINANCIAL PLANNER™ practitioner (CFP®). To qualify as a CFP® practitioner, the planner must take and pass a set of exams on financial planning and have at least three years of experience counseling clients on financial planning matters. To retain certification, the planner must complete a certain number of continuing education credits every two years. She must agree to abide by a professional code of ethics.

The insurance profession's designation for financial planners is called the Chartered Financial Consultant® (ChFC®). Accountants who specialize in providing financial planning advice are called Personal Financial Specialists (PFS). The qualifications and continuing education requirements for both these designations is similar to those required of the CFP® practitioner.

Financial planners are compensated in one of three ways: fee only, commission only or fee and commission.

Fee-only planners charge an hourly fee or flat fee to provide financial planning advice. If you subsequently invest through them, they usually charge a percentage of assets managed.

Fee and commission planners charge hourly rates to provide financial planning advice. If you subsequently invest with them, they may charge you a percentage of the assets managed and/ or they may receive commissions on investments you make.

Commission-only planners charge no fee or a nominal fee and are compensated primarily by the commissions generated by the products you buy from them.

When planning for retirement, we recommend you select a fee-only planner. Your planner will provide you with a contract to sign which will spell out how you will work together. If you don't have a referral source, go to FPAnet.org or LetsMakeAPlan.org to locate a financial planner near you.

RETIREMENT PLANNING SPECIALISTS

Due to increased life expectancy in the United States of America, there are numerous titles which refer to planners who specialize in retirement counseling. Two well-known designations are: the Chartered Retirement Planning Counselor℠ (CRPC®), offered by the College for Financial Planning, and the Retirement Income Certified Professional® (RICP®) offered by the American College of Financial Services. Both require passing an exam and continuing education.

ATTORNEYS

Your lawyer's function is to make sure that you're legally protected. These individuals should have a law degree from an accredited law school and should have passed the bar exam in the state in which they practice. You need to select an attorney specializing in the field in which you need help. For example, use an estate planning lawyer to draw up your estate documents and a real estate lawyer for the sale or purchase of your home.

Typically, lawyers charge an hourly fee, but some may charge a set fee for preparation of certain documents such as your estate planning documents or for a real estate settlement.

Here again, there are also certified elder law attorneys. These lawyers have specialized in elder law for at least five years and passed a written exam covering Medicare and Medicaid regulations (www. nelf.org).

Accountants

The primary role of your accountant is to prepare your taxes each year in a timely fashion and to help you estimate your future tax liability. When planning for retirement, it's important for you to understand how your retirement income will be taxed. The accountant can help you determine how much in taxes should be withheld from your retirement income and whether you should pay estimated quarterly tax payments.

The principal credential in the field of accounting is the Certified Public Accountant (CPA). However, some accountants aren't CPAs but are enrolled agents (EA), who specialize in preparing individual returns and can represent you with the IRS if necessary. The accountant is paid an hourly fee. You will be billed based on how long it takes the accountant to prepare your taxes or retirement planning documents.

Insurance Agents

The primary role of the life insurance agent is to make sure you and your family have sufficient life insurance protection. In addition, she can assist you with health, disability and long-term care insurance. Other insurance agents specialize in auto, household, valuables and umbrella liability insurance.

To be an insurance agent, you need to pass an insurance test and be licensed in the state in which you reside. Some agents have additional training that includes the Chartered Life Underwriter (CLU®) designation, which emphasizes estate planning. Insurance agents are usually compensated by the commissions earned on the policies you buy although there are some agents who practice on a fee-only basis.

*S*TOCKBROKERS

The stockbroker's primary focus is to manage your investments in order to enable you to achieve your financial objectives. She may also be able to buy insurance for you, obtain mortgage financing or prepare a financial plan.

She has passed a comprehensive test on investments called the Series 7. This profession is regulated by the Financial Industry Regulatory Authority (FINRA) and the Securities and Exchange Commission (SEC). She may be compensated by commission only on the investments she makes for you. Alternatively, she now is compensated by a percentage fee of assets managed.

*M*ONEY *M*ANAGERS, INVESTMENT *A*DVISORS, *P*ORTFOLIO *M*ANAGERS

These three titles are interchangeable but this person focuses on managing your investments. Usually she requires a minimum amount of money to manage.

Generally, these advisors charge a percentage of assets managed. Typically, the larger the size of your investment portfolio, the lower percentage fee charged. Frequently there's a minimum annual fee charged.

Bank Trust Officer

The bank trust officer performs the same role as the independent money manager. She manages your investments which are held in a trust. If you are the beneficiary of the trust, the trust officer has two obligations: to produce a competitive level of income for you and, at the same time, to preserve the principal for the trust's ultimate heirs.

The trust officer charges a percentage of assets managed. In addition to the management fee, you also may be charged an administration fee.

Robo And On Line Advice

In recent years, a new group of advisors has developed that pair algorithms for money management with human help. We believe these advisors are best suited to people who have simple financial situations.

Several mutual fund companies offer basic online worksheets to help you figure out whether you have enough money on which to retire. While these calculations can be a good starting point, we think you need more in-depth advice to help you make what can be very complicated decisions.

Realtors

The primary role of the realtor is to assist you should you decide to sell your home, buy a new one or both. She should be a member of the National Association of Realtors® ™. Your realtor will be representing you, but may also represent the other party. Ideally you want your agent to put your interests first. Usually the realtor is paid a percentage of the sales price of the house.

Daily Money Managers

The daily money manager helps you organize your financial paperwork. She can pay your monthly bills, assist with tax records, balance your checkbook, decode your medical bills, file for insurance reimbursement and even negotiate with your creditors.

The certification as a professional daily money manager (DMM) is conferred by the American Association of Daily Money Managers (www.aadmm.com). Typically, they are bonded and insured. Usually the DMM charges an hourly fee which may include travel time to and from your home.

MEDICAL PROFESSIONALS

Physicians

Your primary care physician is an excellent referral source. When you have your annual physical, be sure to bring to her attention all concerns that you may have about any aspect of your health. If you're unsure about what you may need, discuss with her what you're experiencing now that you are retired. She'll work with you to identify what type of specialist is most likely to address your concerns, if you have any. Most physicians have a list of specialists whom they recommend to their patients depending on the matter that needs to be addressed. Every physician belongs to the medical association in the state where she practices. If necessary, these associations are able to provide you with referrals.

Mental Health Professionals

If you're feeling guilty because you're not viewing retirement with the same enthusiasm you think you should, you may want to discuss these feelings with someone in the mental health field. There are many options as discussed below. Like your primary care physician, these professionals will help you determine if what you're experiencing falls within the usual range of emotions experienced when there is a life-changing event on the horizon. If not, she'll discuss with you the appropriate next steps.

Psychiatrists

A psychiatrist is a doctor who has gone to medical school, completed a medical internship and then completed a psychiatric residency, frequently at a hospital specializing in the care of the mentally ill. She may have obtained additional training in a given treatment technique. Psychiatrists, for the most part, are the mental health practitioners currently allowed to prescribe medication to alleviate the debilitating feelings associated with depression, anxiety and other mental or emotional disorders. In a few states, psychologists are also able to prescribe medication after following a specified course of study.

Psychiatrists may also provide psychotherapy on an individual or a group basis. They bill you for their professional time, usually on a fee-per-session basis. The fees for individual sessions are somewhat higher than those for group sessions. Make sure you understand the fee structure and office policies of the individual practitioner you select. The fee structure will vary from state to state.

Psychiatrists provide you with a written description of what they will and will not do, which is known as "informed consent." This information sheet is usually signed by the client, acknowledging her understanding of the process to be undertaken.

Qualified psychiatrists must be licensed in the state in which they practice. Sometimes they are licensed in more than one state. They will have met the requirements to practice medicine with a specialty in psychiatry. Psychiatrists are required, as are all physicians, to remain current by taking courses annually. The requirements are determined by the state in which they practice. In addition, they must abide by a professional code of ethics, as is also true of the other mental health professionals.

PSYCHOLOGISTS

In order to practice as a psychologist, an individual must have completed a four-year college program followed by a three- or four-year doctoral program designed to prepare her for the practice of psychology. The study of normal and abnormal behavior is required and is a component of any such program. After completing this part of the training, those who decide they want to work with people on a therapeutic level move on to an appropriate internship program in an approved treatment facility. Here, psychotherapy training under supervision is provided. Many undergo additional training in a particular therapeutic approach such as relationship and marriage counseling.

In terms of providing therapy to clients, there is considerable similarity between the treatment provided by a psychiatrist and that provided by a psychologist. As previously stated, most psychologists are presently unable to prescribe medication for their clients. Psychologists are the only mental health professionals trained to administer and interpret psychological tests. Psychologists' fee structures are usually configured on an hourly basis. They will clarify the fee structure and office practices either before or at the time of the first session. Like the psychiatrist, they will provide their clients with an "informed consent" form.

Psychologists must be licensed to practice in the state in which they work. They are also required by their state to remain current in their field, in much the same way as are psychiatrists.

Social Workers

Licensed social workers are also required to complete a specific training program. Following the completion of a college course of study, these individuals proceed to a masters level and sometimes a doctoral level program with an emphasis on individual and community services. Social workers also complete an internship in their particular area of interest.

Social workers' fees are based on their background and training. There are always individual differences, but in general, a psychiatrist will charge more than a psychologist and a psychologist will charge more than a social worker. Social workers also have an ongoing education requirement set by the state in which they practice. They too will provide you with written information about their services and what you can expect from the experience.

Pastoral Counselors

If you've been active in an organized religion you may feel comfortable speaking with a pastoral counselor. Pastoral counselors have experience counseling individuals at some crossroad in their lives. i.e., marriage, illness, death, etc. If you feel that it would be helpful to you to consult with someone you respect from the standpoint of your religion, this individual is likely to be helpful. The pastoral counselor has heard all sorts of issues and you should never be embarrassed to make an appointment to discuss a personal matter.

GERIATRIC CARE MANAGERS

A geriatric care manager is a health and human services specialist who acts as a guide and advocate for families caring for older relatives or disabled adults. She has been educated in various fields of human services—social work, psychology, nursing, gerontology—and trained to assess, plan, coordinate, monitor and provide services for the elderly and their families. Advocacy for older adults is a primary function of the geriatric care manager. This person can address a wide variety of care issues. For example she can assess the needs of an aging couple at home and put in place the necessary combination of home health care and transportation. She can also help in selecting an appropriate retirement home.

Certification as a Geriatric Care Manager is granted by the National Academy of Certified Care Managers. Typically, she is paid by the hour. (www.naccm.net)

PHYSICAL THERAPISTS/PERSONAL TRAINERS

Physical therapists are movement experts. They teach patients how to prevent or manage their condition so that they will achieve long-term health benefits. They have an undergraduate degree, which is followed by three years of study to become a Doctor of Physical Therapy (DPT). They have to pass a state administered national exam in order to practice as a physical therapist. If your physician recommends you have physical therapy, then Medicare will pay for a certain number of sessions. Contact www.apta.org to locate a physical therapist in your area or ask your physician for a recommendation.

There are various certifications for personal trainers. The American College of Sports Medicine presents itself as the "gold standard" for trainers. The ACSM certified professionals pass a test, are required to abide by a code of ethics and to keep current in their field by earning continuing education credits. These trainers may be generalists, but some are trained to work with seniors on specific issues like balance. To locate a certified personal trainer in your area contact www.acsm.org.

*N*UTRITIONISTS

Nutritionists are experts in food and nutrition. They can help you select appropriate foods to eat, plan menus and advise you on the health effects of certain foods. They assess your current dietary habits and needs, educate you on healthy eating habits, follow up to make sure menus are working for you and may write reports that document your progress.

To be certified as a nutritionist specialist (CCNS) one must have a masters degree from an accredited university, a 900-hour internship, pass a test administered by the Certified Clinical Nutritionist Board, take ongoing courses to remain current in their field and recertification every five years (ddc@clinicalnutrition.com).

OTHER PEOPLE TO HELP YOUR TRANSITION

*P*ROFESSIONAL *O*RGANIZERS

Professional organizers help you organize your possessions. In other words, if you need to sort out your closet, your garage or your office space, these people can help you. They also might help you get ready for a garage or estate sale. Some of them can help you organize your finances as well, but we think the Daily Money Manager is better suited to that job.

Like most other professions, there is a credential provided by the National Association of Productivity and Organizing professionals (www.napo.net). The professional organizer is paid by the hour. Some offer packages or charge by the project.

Senior Move Managers

The Senior Move Manager helps you declutter and/or reorganize to better help you age in place or move to another location (www.nasmm.org).

Some moving managers charge by the hour, while others offer a package deal. All will provide a written estimate of what their services will cost prior to your hiring them.

Certified Aging In Place Specialists

These specialists can help reconcile the need for a familiar environment with the need to prioritize safety and accessibility. They assist you in making sure your home is safe and comfortable as you age. They develop a plan to modify your home. They often do the remodeling as well, which might include brighter lights, bath and shower grab bars, higher countertops, etc.

The course to receive this designation is offered by the National Association of Home Builders Remodelers. Members of this organization also have to adhere to a code of ethics and continuing education requirements. (www.nahb.com)

Epilogue

Ten Years Later

Catherine Epilogue: Ten Years Later

"Seventy?" Could she really be turning 70 today? It didn't seem possible. She felt fortunate that her law firm didn't have a mandatory retirement age. She still enjoyed her work; she wasn't ready to step down and she could set her own schedule. Her partners valued her contribution to the firm and always respected the work she did. She couldn't believe that it had been 10 years since she and Jordan had begun to address retirement. She couldn't imagine retiring at the age of 60.

Neither she nor Jordan could have predicted that after he was forced to retire as a corporate attorney that he would find himself with a new, successful career in real estate. When Jessica had first suggested that he take a real estate class so that he could join her in her real estate firm he hadn't considered how the job might affect his life. He thought it might be interesting and he did have considerable time on his hands. Initially, he approached this new career casually—until he actually began to do the work and started to make some money. This was a great relief to both Catherine and Jordan given their financial situation. It seemed remarkable to both of them that he now was doing quite well in the real estate market. Clients liked his low-key approach. Basically, he made his own hours and found helping a client find the right home very rewarding. He now even felt somewhat guilty that he and Catherine had bought their Chevy Chase home in such a casual way.

James and Amanda were both married. Jordan and Catherine had participated in the planning of both weddings and really enjoyed spending time with James' in-laws. Unfortunately, they didn't feel the same way about Amanda's in-laws, but they rarely had to see them since they lived out of the area. James and his wife had a two-year-old girl named Melody. She was at that stage where she was saying no to just about everything and anything you asked her to do, but she was undeniably adorable. Catherine and Jordan occasionally baby sat with her when her parents had something special to do or an event to attend. There definitely were times when Catherine couldn't believe she now was a grandmother.

With the help of some caregivers in the last two years of his life, Jordan's dad was able to live with them until he died at the age of 97. The time Jordan was able to spend with his Dad in his last years was very meaningful to both of them. He really was quite functional until the last two years of his life.

Epilogue: Ten Years Later

Her parents were still living and had moved to a retirement community. Although at first they were reluctant to do so, it had turned out well and met their needs. Both her parents had slowed down considerably, and her father suffered from congestive heart failure. Everyone felt good about the fact that they had the services they needed at this time in their lives.

Catherine and Jordan continued to rent out the beach house for two weeks in August even though they no longer really needed to do so. They were pleased that they were able to use this income for travel without dipping into other accounts. They'd continued to work with Joe. They met with him at least once a year and sometimes twice a year if they had some specific questions or concerns with regard to their investments and the retirement plan they had put in place.

In retrospect, Jordan's sudden job loss was a significant turning point in their lives. They realized that they had paid little to no attention as to how they spent their money and were basically operating as individuals and not as a couple. They now spoke regularly about their finances and their mutual financial and lifestyle goals.

Ten years ago, when they were concerned about Jordan obtaining any work, they couldn't have foreseen that not only would he find work but that he would make the money he was now making. He was no longer walking around the house moping, and he had developed new interests and looked forward to his real estate work. He helped James and his wife buy their first house. In addition, Catherine and Jordan agreed it would be a good idea to give them the commission he had earned on the purchase of the house. This would help them to make a larger down payment on the house. This had turned out to be a good experience for all of them.

Catherine still couldn't believe that Jordan had become so interested in healthy eating and food preparation. He read up on the importance of different foods and put together interesting, healthy meals at home several times a week. As for physical activity, they both tried to work out three times a week at the fitness club. They weren't avid exercisers but realized how important it was that they exercise on a regular basis in order to stay fit.

All in all, they were healthier as a couple financially, physically and emotionally. They had an estate plan and a financial plan in place and had expanded their horizons, resulting in a closer relationship and a sense of security with regard to the future.

Emily Epilogue:
Ten Years Later

The smell of coffee brewing in the kitchen greeted Emily as she opened her eyes this morning. Whoever woke up first made the coffee that they then shared to start their day. Had she and Hank actually been married six years? Had it been ten years since she'd stopped working full-time as the executive director for the nonprofit?

She knew she was 74, but she felt less stressed than when she was younger. She couldn't imagine life without Hank. She often felt she was the luckiest woman in the world to have found someone as kind, supportive and caring as Hank. In contrast with her previous marriage, she could breathe and didn't feel she had to be careful not to upset her husband.

So much had happened since she and Hank had agreed to move in together. She loved the condo they'd purchased. Perhaps most importantly, Carter and Louise had gotten married and now had a little boy, Keith, age 3. Emily had made it through Carter's wedding with little difficulty even though Doug had attended with his latest wife, Dawn. She thought he even looked at her with some appreciation, recognizing that she was still slim with a good figure. He, on the other hand, hadn't aged so well!

She and Hank had gotten to know Louise's parents whom they liked. The two families worked together planning the wedding. Carter had matured so much. It was amazing what a difference it made when he felt appreciated by those around him. Louise was great for him. He was a really good husband and dad and had lots of patience with Keith who was very active.

Both she and Hank were now fully retired but were enjoying an active lifestyle. They had a busy social life with both new and old friends. Emily had continued with her yoga classes, which she truly enjoyed. They'd expanded both their joint cooking experiences and added several ethnic restaurants to their existing list of preferred dining places.

They'd remained fairly healthy. Emily had had some minor back problems but nothing chronic or requiring surgical intervention. They both now were good about scheduling annual physicals as well as dental and eye exams. They realized the importance of regular health care to longevity and feeling of well-being.

She and Hank talked about everything from money to what was going on with the children. She sometimes wondered how she'd lived all those years with Doug and allowed him to make all the family decisions.

Hank and Emily continued to divide their household expenses on a two thirds/one third basis. They reviewed their financial situation annually with Shelley. After Keith was born, Emily updated her legal documents again with their estate planning lawyer with whom they had been working since they made the decision to get married.

Hank was very generous and always purchased thoughtful gifts for her. Sometimes for a special occasion, and sometimes just because he wanted to surprise her with something she might have admired in a store. All in all, she realized she was happier now than she'd ever been!

MELISSA EPILOGUE:
TEN YEARS LATER

Another beautiful morning in Sarasota! Melisa realized that it was Saturday and the local farmers market day. She and David continued to spend a good portion of their time in Florida, and the balance of their time was spent in Michigan near their children and grandchildren. Ten years ago, she'd never thought about living in Florida, and now she couldn't imagine how she had lived through all those brutally cold winters and bad weather in Michigan.

Melissa and David were in some ways closer than they had ever been. They spent more time together doing mutually enjoyable activities. They found that they now had time to enjoy each other in a new way. Life was more relaxed, and she wasn't always putting the needs of others first.

She also participated in some individual activities such as the water aerobics class she'd agreed to try with trepidation all those years ago. After the class she and some of the women went out for lunch and some shopping. Occasionally, she and another woman from the class might get together for an activity that was of interest to just the two of them or just to hang out together.

Healthwise, David was thriving in Florida. He played golf on a regular basis with his friends from Michigan. In addition David and a few of his buddies had decided to walk two to three miles three mornings a week. His heart condition had remained stable and although he was now 75, he had no new issues. The stent seemed to be working well. She thought that the regular exercise and the fact that they were more physically active in Florida had contributed to this positive situation.

About five years ago she had had to have a hip replacement. At the time she feared she might never be able to walk again without a limp, but to her surprise, the excellent physical therapy she had had after the surgery, as well as her faithful adherence to a regular exercise routine had resulted in her walking just as well as she ever did. It didn't interfere with any of her activities. She was amazed at all that modern medicine could accomplish.

Hannah hadn't remarried as Melissa thought she would. She'd made great progress at work and had an excellent job with good benefits and a commensurate salary. Since the children were older now, she no longer needed any help with childcare. Tad at 20 was now in his third year at Michigan State where he had gotten a partial scholarship for his soccer skills. His sister, Alexa, was now 18 and getting ready to graduate from high school. She was in the process of looking for colleges, two of which were located in Florida.

Since David and Melissa were in Florida much of the year, Hannah and her brother, Christopher, and his wife, Jean, had become closer. If the families weren't able to gather in Florida for the holidays, they spent them together in Michigan, which they hadn't done previously.

Chris' older daughter was now 25 and about to be married to a great guy she'd met at college. Could Melissa be close to becoming a great-grandmother? That would make her feel really ancient. No point on dwelling on that possibility since they weren't yet married.

Epilogue: Ten Years Later

Melissa had hoped that she could persuade her parents to move down near them in Florida. However, even though her parents enjoyed visiting them in Florida, they had decided to stay in Michigan where they would be close to their friends and grandchildren. They both had some health issues but were still reasonably active. They'd compromised by moving to a retirement community near Hannah. Although they didn't want to move to Florida, they'd visited Melissa and David in Florida annually for a month or so in the winter and had to admit being in the warm weather was a nice alternative to Michigan.

Thanks to David's good financial planning and Ted Johnson's continuing investment advice, they were doing fine money-wise in retirement. Melissa had a greater appreciation of all David had done on their behalf during the years he worked in the auto industry. She understood it all much better now. Despite her initial misgivings, adjusting to David's retirement had turned out to be considerably better than she'd anticipated.

Victoria Epilogue:
Ten Years Later

Today was graduation day at the university. Victoria realized that it had been ten years since she'd walked with her fellow professors toward the podium at her last graduation ceremony. As she reflected on the past ten years, she realized that her life in retirement was very full in ways she never could have imagined.

She was most grateful she'd remained in remission from her breast cancer diagnosis for all this time. She was as active as she chose to be. She maintained her exercise regimen and monitored her diet so that she ate well-balanced meals. She monitored her weight and was proud to see that it had remained the same over the years. She'd joined a running club and even participated in a couple of local mini marathons.

The first trip Victoria had led to Mexico had been very successful and well received by both the students and the administration. As a result, the people at the university had approached her and asked her if she would be willing to lead one trip each academic year to South America. She was thrilled with the offer and accepted it with alacrity. She loved spending time with the students on these trips. She really enjoyed sharing her interest in that part of the world with them. She was gratified that they always seemed enthusiastic and receptive. She only recently stopped leading these trips.

She and her nephew Rodney had taken two archeological trips together over the years, one to Peru and the other to Mexico. While these trips primarily were educational, they'd had a wonderful time. They made new friends, ate the local food and drank the local beers and wine. It was hard to believe that now Rodney was 35 and married with a son and a baby on the way!

Victoria had maintained her friendship with some of the members of the writers group. She enjoyed sharing various activities with them, such as plays, lectures, and concerts. She found these friendships were more meaningful to her now that she was no longer involved in her university life. She'd expanded her involvement with the theatre group by taking on small acting parts as well as backstage work. Victoria really liked the people and thought the feeling was reciprocal.

The work with Dr Ross's patients, which she had taken on at his request, had really grown. She'd started by talking to four women that first year. She'd maintained her relationship with two of them and they'd formed a group, making their services available on a pro bono basis not only to Dr Ross's patients but also to other doctors in his group. They called themselves the "Caring Survivors" and met regularly. They made sure that they always had someone available for a patient in need of their services. It was hard to explain the close bond she'd formed with these patients. She was grateful to be able to give back in such a meaningful way.

Financially she was doing fine. Her decision to stay in her home in Berkeley and making the basement into a rental apartment was the right one. It had more than paid for itself and provided her with some extra income as well as companionship.

Victoria could barely remember a time when she didn't have a basement apartment in her townhouse. Three years ago, she'd rented to Justine, a female professor who was new to the state and the university. They'd really connected to the point that they'd become good friends and attended some events together from time to time. Victoria also appreciated having Justine there who could care for her current cat, Cinders, when she went to San Francisco.

Initially, Victoria had been somewhat worried about how she would adjust to retirement. She had been so absorbed in her job as a professor for so many years, that she wasn't sure how she would adapt to having so much free time. It turned out she shouldn't have worried. She was involved in so many different activities, that she was almost busier than when she was at the university, which hardly seemed possible. Ten years ago, she couldn't have envisioned having such a rich life in retirement.

Appendices

APPENDIX A

Age To Receive Full Social Security Benefits

(Called "full retirement age" or "normal retirement age.")

1937 or earlier	65
1938	65 and 2 months
1939	65 and 4 months
1940	65 and 6 months
1941	65 and 8 months
1942	65 and 10 months
1943–1954	66
1955	66 and 2 months
1956	66 and 4 months
1957	66 and 6 months
1958	66 and 8 months
1959	66 and 10 months
1960 and later	67

If you were born on January 1st of any year you should refer to the previous year. (If you were born on the 1st of the month, Social Security figures your benefit (and your full retirement age) as if your birthday was in the previous month.)

Source: https://www.ssa.gov/

APPENDIX B

IRS LIFE EXPECTANCY TABLES FOR REQUIRED MINIMUM DISTRIBUTIONS (AS OF 2019)

Table III: (Uniform Lifetime)

For Use by: Unmarried Owners;
Married Owners Whose Spouses Aren't More Than 10 Years Younger; and
Married Owners Whose Spouses Aren't the Sole Beneficiaries of Their IRAs

Age	Current Uniform Lifetime Table Table III: (Uniform Lifetime)		Proposed New Uniform Lifetime Table	
	Current Uniform Table RMD Factor	*Current RMD as a % of Account Balance*	*New Uniform Table RMD Factor*	*New RMD as a % of Account Balance*
70	27.4	3.65%	29.1	3.44%
71	26.5	3.78%	28.2	3.55%
72	25.6	3.91%	27.3	3.67%
73	24.7	4.05%	26.4	3.79%
74	23.8	4.21%	25.5	3.93%
75	22.9	4.37%	24.6	4.07%
76	22	4.55%	23.7	4.22%
77	21.2	4.72%	22.8	4.39%
78	20.3	4.93%	21.9	4.57%
79	19.5	5.13%	21	4.77%
80	18.7	5.35%	20.2	4.96%
81	17.9	5.59%	19.3	5.19%
82	17.1	5.85%	18.4	5.44%
83	16.3	6.14%	17.6	5.69%
84	15.5	6.46%	16.8	5.96%
85	14.8	6.76%	16	6.25%

Age	Current Uniform Lifetime Table Table III: (Uniform Lifetime)		Proposed New Uniform Lifetime Table	
	Current Uniform Table RMD Factor	Current RMD as a % of Account Balance	New Uniform Table RMD Factor	New RMD as a % of Account Balance
86	14.1	7.10%	15.2	6.58%
87	13.4	7.47%	14.4	6.95%
88	12.7	7.88%	13.6	7.36%
89	12	8.34%	12.9	7.76%
90	11.4	8.78%	12.1	8.27%
91	10.8	9.26%	11.4	8.78%
92	10.2	9.81%	10.8	9.26%
93	9.6	10.42%	10.1	9.91%
94	9.1	10.99%	9.5	10.53%
95	8.6	11.63%	8.9	11.24%
96	8.1	12.35%	8.3	12.05%
97	7.6	13.16%	7.8	12.83%
98	7.1	14.09%	7.3	13.70%
99	6.7	14.93%	6.8	14.71%
100	6.3	15.88%	6.4	15.63%
101	5.9	16.95%	5.9	16.95%
102	5.5	18.19%	5.6	17.86%
103	5.2	19.24%	5.2	19.24%
104	4.9	20.41%	4.9	20.41%
105	4.5	22.23%	4.6	21.74%
106	4.2	23.81%	4.3	23.26%
107	3.9	25.65%	4.1	24.40%
108	3.7	27.03%	3.9	25.65%
109	3.4	29.42%	3.7	27.03%
110	3.1	32.26%	3.5	28.58%
111	2.9	34.49%	3.4	29.42%

	Current Uniform Lifetime Table Table III: (Uniform Lifetime)		Proposed New Uniform Lifetime Table	
Age	Current Uniform Table RMD Factor	Current RMD as a % of Account Balance	New Uniform Table RMD Factor	New RMD as a % of Account Balance
112	2.6	38.47%	3.2	31.25%
113	2.4	41.67%	3.1	32.26%
114	2.1	47.62%	3	33.34%
115	1.9	52.64%	2.9	34.49%
116	1.9	52.64%	2.8	35.72%
117	1.9	52.64%	2.7	37.04%
118	1.9	52.64%	2.5	40.00%
119	1.9	52.64%	2.3	43.48%
120 and over	1.9	52.64%	2	50.00%
Source: © Michael Kitces, www.kitces.com				

Note: There is a separate table that you have to refer to if your spouse is more than 10 years younger and is the sole beneficiary of an IRA. Table II (Joint Life and Last Survivor Expectancy). Please visit https://www.irs.gov for additional information.

Source: https://www.irs.gov

Due to the Coronavirus, all required minimum distributions were waived for the taxable year 2020.

Appendix C

2020 Federal Income Tax Brackets

*Each year the IRS typically changes tax brackets slightly.
Here is the breakdown for taxes due in April 2021.*

Tax Brackets for Single Filers

Tax Rate	Taxable Income Bracket	Tax Owed
10%	$0 to $9,875	10% of the taxable income
12%	$9,876 to $40,125	$988 plus 12% of the amount over $9,875
22%	$40,126 to $85,525	$4,618 plus 22% of the amount over $40,125
24%	$85,526 to $163,300	$14,606 plus 24% of the amount over $85,525
32%	$163,301 to $207,350	$33,272 plus 32% of the amount over $163,300
35%	$207,351 to $518,400	$47,368 plus 35% of the amount over $207,350
37%	$518,401 or more	$156,235 plus 37% of the amount over $518,400

Tax Brackets for Married—Filing Jointly

Tax Rate	Taxable Income Bracket	Tax Owed
10%	$0 to $19,750	10% of the taxable income
12%	$19,751 to $80,250	$1,975 plus 12% of the amount over $19,750
22%	$80,251 to $171,050	$9,235 plus 22% of the amount over $80,250
24%	$171,051 to $326,600	$29,211 plus 24% of the amount over $171,050
32%	$326,601 to $414,700	$66,543 plus 32% of the amount over $326,600
35%	$414,701 to $622,050	$94,735 plus 35% of the amount over $414,700
37%	$622,051 or more	$167,308 plus 37% of the amount over $622,050

Tax Brackets for Married—Filing Separately

Tax Rate	Taxable Income Bracket	Tax Owed
10%	$0 to $9,875	10% of the taxable income
12%	$9,876 to $40,125	$988 plus 12% of the amount over $9,875
22%	$40,126 to $85,525	$4,618 plus 22% of the amount over $40,125
24%	$85,526 to $163,300	$14,606 plus 24% of the amount over $85,525
32%	$163,301 to $207,350	$33,272 plus 32% of the amount over $163,300
35%	$207,351 to $311,025	$47,368 plus 35% of the amount over $207,350
37%	$311,026 or more	$83,654 plus 37% of the amount over $311,025

Tax Brackets for Head of Household

Tax Rate	Taxable Income Bracket	Tax Owed
10%	$0 to $14,100	10% of the taxable income
12%	$14,101 to $53,700	$1,410 plus 12% of the amount over $14,100
22%	$53,701 to $85,500	$6,162 plus 22% of the amount over $53,700
24%	$85,501 to $163,300	$13,158 plus 24% of the amount over $85,500
32%	$163,301 to $207,350	$31,830 plus 32% of the amount over $163,300
35%	$207,351 to $518,400	$45,926 plus 35% of the amount over $207,350
37%	$518,401 or more	$154,794 plus 37% of the amount over $518,400

Source: https://www.irs.gov

Some Final Notes

*T*hanks for reading our book! If you loved the book and have a moment to spare, we would really appreciate a short review as this helps new readers find our books.

Please visit our website, *https://your-nextchapter.com* for links to the worksheets contained in the book, as well as our newsletter, blogs and current information regarding issues that are relevant to planning your successful retirement.

This book is available at special quantity discounts. For more information please contact us at *yournextchapterauthors@gmail.com*

About the Authors

ALEXANDRA ARMSTRONG, CFP®

Alexandra Armstrong, CFP®, was one of the first women in the country to become a CERTIFIED FINANCIAL PLANNER™ practitioner (CFP®). In addition, she is a Chartered Retirement Planning Counselor℠ (CRPC®). Alex serves as chairman emeritus of Armstrong, Fleming & Moore, Inc., a financial planning firm based in Washington, DC, which she founded in 1983. Her clients include single women, dual-income couples and those close to retirement as well as those already retired.

Alex has held leadership roles at several nonprofit organizations. She served as the chairman of the Financial Planning Association (first female), Foundation for Financial Planning, the Boy Scouts National Capital Area Council (first female) and the International Womens Forum of Washington, DC. She was treasurer of Reading is Fundamental as well as the DC Police Foundation.

Alex has written a monthly financial planning column for Better Investing magazine for the past forty years. She is coauthor of "On Your Own; A Widow's Passage to Emotional and Financial Well-Being," now in its fifth edition. She has been quoted in virtually every major U.S. financial publication and has appeared on numerous national television programs, including CBS This Morning, Good Morning America and Wall$treet Week.

Alex offers securities through her broker dealer, Commonwealth Financial Network, Member FINRA/ SIPC, a Registered Investment Adviser. Her firm is Armstrong, Fleming & Moore, Inc., which is a Registered Investment Adviser. Advisory services and fixed insurance products and services offered by Armstrong Fleming & Moore, Inc., are separate and unrelated to Commonwealth.

Mary R. Donahue, PH.D.

Dr Mary R. Donahue has a successful psychology practice in the Washington, DC, metropolitan area. Her practice is primarily focused on families in crisis, domestic abuse and women addressing life altering issues such as relationships, career development, and loss.

Mary's commitment to women's issues has led her to speak with regularity to both professional and lay audiences. This includes educating the judiciary and professional groups such as the American Bar Association, local county Bar Associations and the Association of Family and Conciliatory courts. She has been a contributor to the Washingtonian magazine and spoken on both radio and television shows with regard to these matters.

Dr Donahue is a member of the American Psychological Association and the Maryland Psychological Association. She is the coauthor of "On Your Own: a Widow's Passage to Emotional and Financial Well-Being," now in its fifth edition. She is also the coauthor of a children's book titled "What's My Job," written for youngsters at a point of transition in their lives.

Acknowledgments

Our thanks to the following people who contributed their expertise to this book:

Julie Andrews CFP®, Elissa Buie CFP®, Marc Charon, Jon Dauphine, Marilyn Dimitroff CFP®, Valerie Donely, Debra Englander, Rachel A. Fitzpatrick, BCC™, Betsy Fleming, Ryan Fleming CFP®, Jack Gaffney, Mary Garrard, Laurie Harmon, Psy.D, Carl Holubowich CFP®, Gregory S Hinkson CFP®, Michael E. Kitces, MSFS, MTAX, CFP®, Sydney LeBlanc, Lauren Mariano, Sumedha Malhotra CFP®, Mary Moore CFP®, Susan and David Parry, Christopher Rivers CFP®, Marilyn Salinger, Terry Savage, Katie Votava, Krista Weaver

Resources

FINANCIAL

Anthony, Mitch. *The New Retirementality*. Hoboken, New Jersey; John Wiley & Sons, Inc 4th Edition 2014

Hurme, Sally Balch, *Get the most out of Retirement: A checklist for happiness, Health, Purpose & Financial Security*, Chicago, American Bar Association/AARP, *2017*

Johnson, Marni, *Downsizing the Family Home: What to Toss, what to Keep*, AARP/Sterling, 2016

Kiplinger's Retirement Planning 2019 (published annually in April) by Kiplinger Washington Editors, Inc.)

Kiplinger's Retirement Report—a monthly newsletter published by Kiplinger Washington Editors.Inc.

Savage, Terry. *The Savage Truth on Money*, Third Edition, New York NY; John Wiley & Sons. 2020

Sullivan, Greg. *Retirement Fail*: The 9 Reasons People Flunk Postwork Life & How to Ace your Own, New York, NY; John Wiley & Sons. 2019

Personal Growth

Culinane, Jan, AARP, The Single Woman's Guide to Retirement, Hoboken, NJ; John Wiley and Sons. 2012

Nelson, John E.and Bolles, Richard N, *What Color is your Parachute for Retirement*: Planning a Prosperous, Healthy, and Happy Future. Berkeley, CA : Potter/Ten Speed/Harmony/Rodale. 2010

Schofield, George H Ph.D, *How do I Get There From Here*: Planning for Retirement When the Old Rules NO Longer Apply, New York, NY: AMACOM. 2017

Smith, Dr Rita, *Empty Nest, Empty Desk, What's Next*: How Boomer Professional Women are Reinventing their Retirement, USA; Outskirts Press 2018

Thurman, Eric, *Thrive in Retirement*: Simple Secrets for Being Happy for the Rest of Your Life, New York, NY; Waterbrook a division of Penguin Random House. 2019

Tyson, Eric and Carlson, Bob. *Retirement Planning*, Hoboken, NJ; John Wiley and Sons 2018

Zelinski, Ernie J, *How to Retire Happy, Wild, and Free*: Retirement Wisdom that you Wont Get from Your Financial Advisor, Edmonton. AB, Canada, Visions International Publishing. 2015

Index